AF351423

Table of Contents

Power Play: Great Engine Wars in Commercial Aviation – GE Aviation, Pratt & Whitney, Rolls Royce, Safran

From the Dawn of Jet Age through the End of Cold War

@9000RPM Publishing Works

RAJAT NARANG

Published by: @9000RPM Works

Cover Page Design: Canva.com

Cover Image Credits: Nikita Grishin, Image ID: 10320757

Image Source: Pexels.com

Disclaimer

The Author does not have any kind of financial investments, direct business associations or financial stakes of any sort in any of the companies included & mentioned in this work. It does not promote or endorse any particular company or industry player & its products over others in any manner whatsoever. The overall scope & directional reference compass of this work primarily is the global narrow body aircraft market with focus on relative, comparative analysis from a longitudinal strategy perspective under the purview of the prevailing strategic & operating context.

The analysis has been purely anchored on factual evidences available in the public domain based information sources and utmost effort has been made to ensure fair play to present the most objective view of reality against the backdrop & in light of the available facts rather than taking a biased view skewed towards any of the industry behemoths covered. The approach taken, thus, is intended to clearly avoid the scope for straying towards the dark zone marked by deception, subterfuge & sabotage tactics, black ops, undercover missions, propaganda and/or shows of mudslinging.

The opinions expressed throughout are purely author's personal and the views & judgments presented are neither directed or targeted at anyone nor meant as pontification of any sort and are solely based on objective assessment of prevailing situations, decisions & outcomes. The names of engines, airplane programs, products, systems and/or brand names mentioned wherever through the work are intellectual property of their respective owners and their mention has been done only & purely for information & creative purposes and it does not indicate or reflect and should not be construed as any kind of promotion or endorsement of any kind.

The lenses used to view and analyze the series of events & key junctures have primarily been of strategy rather than just history which invariably led to limiting the scope for deep dives to areas & angles relevant from the strategy perspective. It is also not intended as a technology/technical guide with the inclusion of some technical aspects & performance parameters for analysis done purely from the relative strategy perspective.

The information and facts contained herein are believed to be correct at the time of publication but cannot be guaranteed. All the information presented has been derived from reliable sources, reasonably verified & has been presented purely & solely for informational purposes only. The views expressed throughout are based on broad analysis & assessments only and thus should not be substituted for professional advice & opinion of any kind prior to decision-making. The author expressly disclaims any and all liability to any person or entity pertaining to potential outcomes or consequences of any decisions or actions taken based on the contents of this publication.

The analysis presented cites quotes, comments, statements and very short excerpts from public reports; derived from public domain based information sources; originating from & pertaining to industry leaders, senior company executives, industry & company analysts, journalists, aviation authorities, industry bodies & other authority figures from the commercial aviation industry with reference to particular situational contexts with citations, proper attribution & due credits provided under fair terms of use. The incorporation of these has been done throughout purely to provide readers with actual prevailing viewpoints, opinions & industry stakeholders' take on the specific operating and/or strategic context being analyzed as contextual evidences for the lines of analysis presented, angles of view taken and positions adopted on strategy moves as well as inferences & conclusions drawn. The approach has also been taken for the readers to be able to fairly construct the contours of the subject matter clearly, review them, be able to form their own unbiased judgments, opinions & viewpoints and be able to explore the subject further by treading along the provided pathway & digging deeper.

The presented content contains generic information only and is not suitable for addressing specific or particular circumstances of any specific case or scenario. The content, thus, is not intended to be used as a basis for taking decisions of commercial or any other nature. The authors and the publisher disclaim all liabilities originating from the outcomes of the application of the contents in real-life scenarios without duly conducting thorough due diligence and without seeking professional advice & opinion from relevant subject matter experts.

ACKNOWLEDGMENTS

Sincere thanks, due regards and special acknowledgements to all the well known as well as unsung aviation engineers, airplane designers, test pilots & pilots, adventurers, entrepreneurs, industry personnel, enthusiasts and aerospace journalists, analysts as well as publishers who have dedicated their lives to shaping the industry's evolution through time, those doing it at the moment and the ones yet to come to take on the mantle and steer this wonderful journey forward!

Let's keep the 'Spirit of Adventure' going!

Bypass Ratio (BPR): In a turbofan (bypass) engine, the bypass ratio is a comparison or ratio between the mass flow rate of air drawn into the engine (through the fan disk that goes *around* the engine core **but not to the gas generator**) with the mass flow rate of the air that goes *through* the engine core, including, the gas generator. In an engine with a bypass ratio of 10:1, for every 11 units of air drawn into the engine, 10 will bypass the engine core and 1 will go through it, as per Skybrary.

Engine Pressure Ratio (EPR): EPR is the total pressure ratio across a jet engine, measured as the ratio of the total pressure at the exit of the propelling nozzle divided by the total pressure at the entry to the compressor.

Fan Pressure Ratio (FPR): A ratio of the fan's discharge pressure to the fan's inlet pressure.

Thrust-specific Fuel Consumption (TSFC): TSFC or SFC for thrust engines (e.g. turbojets, turbofans, ramjets, rockets, etc.) is the mass of fuel needed to provide the net thrust for a given period e.g. lb/(h·lbf) (pounds of fuel per hour-pound of thrust).

Mean Time Between Failures (MTBF): MTBF is the average time between repairable failures of an engine or its parts. The metric is used to track both the availability and reliability of a product. A higher MTBF value indicates a more reliable engine.

Mean Time Between Removals (MTBR): A ratio calculated by dividing the total engine flying hours accrued in a period (Time on Wing) by the number of incidents of engine removals (scheduled as well as unscheduled) that occurred during the same period.

Preface

The Wright Brothers' dream of flying like birds in their powered Wright Flyer was realized in 1903 by a 12 Hp, all Aluminum gasoline engine generating a thrust output of mere 100 pound force. Humanity, thus, has made giant strides & taken multiple technological leaps within a span of a century and two decades since then with today's giant aviation turbofan engines capable of generating over 100,000 pound force thrust levels. The journey from 100 lbf of thrust to 100,000 lbf of thrust, thus, has been fascinating indeed and full of technological challenges & hurdles for the mankind.

The biggest technological leap, however, was made in the 1930s, in form of the transition from piston powered engines to gas turbines, and was provided by the raging crucibles of war and the extremely powerful forces of competition, as usual, with the World War II proving to be the most fertile ground for germination of seeds of radical technological evolution. This was the tipping point for aviation and arrived in form of the development of gas turbines for military aviation applications in the late 1930s across both Germany and the Great Britain and quickly & effectively culminated into full scale commercial production & introduction of jet powered fighter aircrafts in 1944 by both sides delivering game changing capabilities.

The concept of gas turbines was there in theory for a long time with patents being granted for it as early as the 18th century. However, it was not realized until the third decade of the 20th century with the commissioning of the first constant flow industrial gas turbine in the U.S. at an oil refinery based in Pennsylvania in 1936.

Gas turbines, essentially, use kerosene as fuel, unlike piston engines, which run on regular gasoline and generate huge amounts of power for a broad range of applications, including, aviation, marine ships, power generation, aircraft APUs and even transmissions of tanks, with the U.S. Army's M1A1 Abrams being a prominent example. However, they are fuel guzzlers and meant for large applications primarily as they can't match the fuel efficiency of gasoline or diesel powered internal combustion engines used routinely for automotive applications. It was a huge problem during the early years of their development which was ultimately tackled & resolved by the engineers.

The jet engine heralded the dawn of commercial aviation's jet age in the post World War II years which effectively brought in a revolution in air travel with the possibility of reaching any part of the globe from anywhere within 24 hours becoming an operational reality.

Rolls Royce, GE Aviation and Pratt & Whitney were the early pioneers in the development of commercial jet engines from their military counterparts and have remained as the top players in the global commercial aviation propulsion market even after 7+ decades of its existence. This is the analysis-based story of those complex strategy choices, decisions & moves made by these leading turbofan engine OEMs amid the heat of the raging battles and the myopic errors caused by the prevailing fog-of-war and their eventual outcomes & repercussions. The analysis also factors in the critical & pivotal role played by the prevailing market forces, macroeconomic trends and lastly chance which collectively proved to be the presiding, ultimate judges with their judgments & verdicts ultimately determining the fates as well as destinies of engine programs as well as the OEMs making them.

It is also the story of path-breaking innovations, products & technologies, some of which, aided by the prevailing favorable market forces, disrupted the commercial aviation market fundamentally while carving a niche for themselves initially & ultimately going on to virtual market dominance. However, there were some others as well, which, despite of being disruptive, were way ahead of their time and were ultimately discarded by the market forces owing to being out of alignment with current market realities of the time only to re-emerge, reincarnated in an entirely new form now, incredibly, to solve complex sustainability challenges and to shape a new, sustainable future for commercial aviation, chosen to be resurrected, ironically, by the very same market forces which had once sealed their fates...

Chapter I

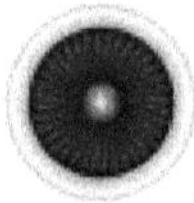

The 'Jet' Engine Saga

It was January 30, 1933 and a man, who was a former corporal and had fought for Germany in World War I, had just made his way into the Reichstag as the new chancellor of Germany. His name was Adolf Hitler and he was being hailed as a savior by the German people, who had been somehow looking for a miracle of hope. They had been reeling under the pressure of severe economic hardships & pressures, following the outbreak of the 'Great Depression', with the situation further exacerbated by the demands being made by the allies of Germany, which included reparations for having waged the war (WWI). All of it, collectively, had caused a subsequent, massive economic meltdown and de-valuation of the German currency under the reign of Field Marshal Hindenburg who had been appointed as the second elected president of the German Weimar republic earlier in 1925.

Having promised grand visions of Germany's resurgence and restoration of the old, lost glory of the bygone era to the German people; along with malice, hatred & vengeance towards all those who had scripted the nation's fall from glory, following the ignominious defeat in the World War I; he rebooted his administrative & military machinery and reoriented it towards military ascendancy. The moves were thoroughly planned, seamlessly coordinated and backed by strong R&D & production outlays for weapons and defense industrial base renaissance, geared ultimately towards pursuing an agenda of hatred and revenge directed at all other inhabitants of the European continent.

Within a span of 5 years, the defense industrial base revamp, revitalization & rearmament of the German armed forces and other cogs in his war machinery had been completed and on September 01, 1939, the monster of war was, thus, formally unleashed by Hitler on Europe with the invasion of Poland which marked the official beginning of the second major war in Europe, exactly 2 decades after the end of World War I.

Pursuing advanced technologies as well as lethal weapons of war and their development for mass destruction and for an overmatch over adversaries, was an integral component of his grand visions which effectively manifested in the form of multiple technological breakthroughs, including, the development of world's first jet engine-powered military fighters and V1 & V2 rockets, which were the precursor of modern age missiles.

Jet Engine and World War II – The Genesis

The jet engine essentially is a gas turbine; traditionally used for power generation and naval ships propulsion; used for aviation applications and its invention marked aviation's transition from piston powered airplanes to the much faster, gas turbines powered airplanes during the World War II.

Historically, the patent for usage of gas turbines for aviation applications was filed in 1921, by French national Maxime Guillaume, who had theorized it. However, British engineer, inventor and Royal Air Force Officer Sir Frank Whittle is duly considered as the father of the jet engine as he had filed the patent for the design of a functional turbojet engine in 1930 and he subsequently developed a prototype for the world' first turbojet engine in 1937.

However, the German engineers turned out to be the first ones to have built the first flying jet plane powered by a turbojet engine. It was the Heinkel He 178, built by Hans von Ohain, who worked for the German aircraft designer & manufacturer Dr. Ernst Heinkel. He 178 was an experimental airplane which flew on August 27, 1939. Sir Frank Whittle, however, managed to conduct the maiden flight of his turbojet engine only in 1941 owing to his personal health issues at the time.

German engine designer, Anselm Franz, improvised the jet engine design further by building upon Ohain's work for usage in jet fighters. It led to the development of the Me 262, with Me referring to Messerschmitt, the German aircraft manufacturing company named after its chief designer Willy Messerschmitt. The Me 262 was the world's first operational jet engine powered fighter aircraft to have flown during World War II. It conducted its maiden flight, powered by a pair of Junkers Jumo turbojet engines producing a thrust output of 1,980 lbf, on July 18, 1942.

Developed as an interceptor, it however, consumed a lot of fuel and spent more time on the ground than in the air for a multitude of reasons, including, the demand for it to be converted for usage as a fighter bomber rather than as an interceptor, apart from the reliability and engine issues faced by it. It finally became operational with the Luftwaffe as a light bomber, reconnaissance and experimental night fighter only in the mid-1944.

On the allied side, the Whittle engine was used by British engineers to power the Gloster Meteor, which became the first allied jet powered aircraft used in active combat operations during World War II, after its first flight in 1943 and subsequent utilization by the Royal Air Force (RAF) for combat duty, a year later in July 1944, as a combat fighter.

The Comet was powered by a pair of Whittle W.2/700 engines initially & later with Rolls Royce's Derwent 8 turbojet engines and had a better thrust-to-weight ratio and a higher service ceiling of 43,000 ft. as against Me 262's 37,000 ft.

The Comet had been developed originally an interceptor but due to its limited relative speed vs. the Me 262, it was never used in combat operations over Germany. The Me 262, in fact, was almost 150 km/hr. faster and more heavily armed than any Allied fighter aircraft deployed across the European theater during the war.

The Whittle engine's design & technology was shared by Great Britain with the United States, which led to the development & production of jet engines in America by General Electric (GE) at its Lynn, MA based facility, which led to the emergence of America's first experimental jet powered fighter, in the form of Bell XP-59 Airacomet, which was an experimental aircraft (as indicated by its XP initials).

The British had, in fact, shipped actual, working Whittle engines to the U.S., which reached GE for redesign and operational utilization by a team of GE employees, nicknamed & referred collectively to as the "Hush-Hush Boys"[32], who completed its test firing on April 18, 1942. In fact, Sir Frank Whittle also made a visit to the GE facility in Lynn later and had discussions with GE engineers regarding utilization of the engine for aerial combat.

The GE-produced engine became the J31 turbojet engine. However, it was not used on the XP-59 program as the XP-59 was underpowered and it was, subsequently, used as a trainer aircraft to train fighter pilots. The J31 was used, instead, on the Lockheed-built P-80 Shooting Star, developed by Skunk Works under the legendary aircraft designer & engineer Kelly Johnson, and was delivered in January 1945, within just 143 days from the start of design process in 1944. However, American jets witnessed very limited utilization and almost nil combat action, as the World War II quickly ended in 1945.

The Dawn of Commercial Jet Age

Following the end of World War II, efforts started towards utilization of turbojet engines for commercial applications. The British, with their clear head start as the pioneers of the jet engine, also became instrumental in heralding the dawn of the jet age, i.e. in the development of turbojets- powered commercial airplanes for transporting people.

De Havilland DH.106 Comet 1 prototype, thus, became the world's first jet engine-powered commercial aircraft to have undertaken its maiden flight in 1949, powered by 4 De Havilland Ghost turbojet engines. It subsequently entered commercial service in 1952 with the British European Airways (BEA).

However, its ticket to fame was relatively short lived as the Comet 1 had to be extensively redesigned, following multiple air-crashes owing to metal fatigue, an unknowm phenomenon at the time. A subsequent, redesigned & mature Comet 4 prototype took-off in 1958 and was successful in overcoming the shortcomings of earlier prototypes. The Comet, however, provided a number of very useful lessons to other airplane manufacturers of the era on a wide range of relatively lesser known aerodynamic phenomenon, issues as well as effects.

The French were the second to catch the jet wave with their SE 210 Caravelle, developed & produced by the French companies SNCASE & Sud Aviaton respectively, using design elements & components made originally by them for De Havilland. The Caravelle had undertaken its maiden flight, powered by Rolls Royce Avon turbojet engines (which powered the type's initial variants), in 1955 and entered commercial service with the SAS in 1959.

The Americans, however, boarded the commercial jet age only in 1958 onboard a Boeing 707 commercial aircraft operated by Pan Am and powered by a quartet of Pratt & Whitney's JT3C turbojet engines, taking off successfully from New York.

The early turbojet engines, however, were very loud and were also deemed to be way-more noisier than their predecessors, the propeller powered aircrafts, especially in the U.S. market. The commercial aircraft manufacturers in the U.S., namely, Boeing and Douglas, thus, were being subjected to significant regulatory tussle and stringent operational grind lasting for a span of almost 2 years, from 1956 to 1958, over potential noise issues emanating from operations of jet aircrafts and the nuisance it would have created for residents staying in the vicinity of the airports. The operational clearance for the maiden flight of Pan Am's 707 eventually came in early October 1958 which effectively also was America's tryst with the Jet Age...(more on that interesting story in Chapter 9).

Chapter II

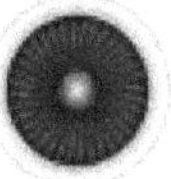

An 'Extraordinary' Decade

On May 1st, 1960 a major international crisis erupted at the peak of the Cold War, which had typically been characterized by frequent, ongoing & simmering tensions between the two superpowers competing for supremacy in a typical bipolar world set-up, in which, the fears of a nuclear Armageddon were absolutely real and the end of human civilization on planet Earth being an everyday possibility with talks of nuclear apocalypse being a daily affair and part of everyday life. As President Kennedy aptly put it, it was a "Sword of Damocles hanging by the slenderest thread".

Almost all morning newspapers of the World had almost the same headline on that Labor Day of 1960, which extensively covered the shooting down of an American U2 spy plane[1] by the Soviet Union's Air Defenses while flying over its sovereign territory. The shooting down had also led to the U.S. pilot, Francis Gary Powers, getting captured alive by the Soviets after he ejected from his U2 deep behind enemy lines after being hit by a Soviet Buck-8 SAM.

The incident had brought the existence of the highly-classified U2 spy plane program into the public eye for the very first time and, unsurprisingly, created an international furore. The U2 incident also caused a fracas between the two arch-rivals, the U.S. & the U.S.S.R, at the Paris Summit[2], which was to be held exactly 19 days later, wherein, the U.S. President Dwight D. Eisenhower faced the Soviet premier Nikita Khrushchev with the latter almost charging out of the summit in a fit of rage while blaming the Americans vehemently for spying activities, which, effectively had torpedoed the Paris summit.

What ensued was a series of hectic & elaborate diplomatic parleys, held between the two superpowers over the following years, under the aegis of the United Nations, for the release of Powers, who had been held in Soviet captivity for 3 years. However, ultimately, he was released with the incident further exacerbating the already bitter relations between the arch-rivals while effectively bringing them further down to an all-time low. The incident had just been preceded by the dawn of the 'thermonuclear arms race' between the rivals following the testing of a hydrogen bomb by the Soviet Union in 1959, thereby, effectively taking the nuclear arms race between the two superpowers to the next level.

Retrospectively, there are just two words to most accurately describe the onset of the 1960s decade for the world, and they are 'Explosive' & 'Revolutionary'. A decade, which was extraordinary by any means & stretch of imagination given the number of high intensity, extraordinary set of events it packed within its fold.

The U2 incident was followed by another heated encounter & exchange, which almost brought the world to the verge of a nuclear flashpoint, for the first time since the dawn of the nuclear age. It was the 1962's Cuban missile crisis, with the U.S and the U.S.S.R, almost slugging it out in the nuclear mode, with the nuclear flashpoint & apocalypse, somehow averted, fortunately. The Cuba crisis gave way to the official blowing of the war trumpet by the arch-rivals once again, with the battle theater this time being Southeast Asia, in form of the onset of the Vietnam War in 1965, which went on for almost a decade.

The war in Vietnam had a huge & indelible impression, as well as impact on the psyche of that generation, as highlighted & epitomized by waves of massive anti-war protests & the anti-establishment culture which followed, conjoined by the onset of hippie movement and social unrest over racial issues, spearheaded by the civil rights movement as its apotheosis. It was followed by a series of political assassinations rounding off a tumultuous decade which turned out to be and, in fact, was almost a conflagration of repressed, charged & flared up emotions.

On the business side of things, these waves of mass unrests & the accompanying spirit of rebellion, seemingly, also made their way inside corporate America and effectively provided tailwinds for their expression, in the form, of development & introduction of some truly radical product designs & maverick products, which subsequently were huge successful and ultimately went on to achieve almost a cult status, with some of them even still very much around in the 21st century.

The long list of these products, undoubtedly, was led by the introduction of the Mustang by Ford Motor Corporation in 1966, which very effectively captured the zeitgeist of the unusual times, fleshed it out and almost embodied this spirit, quintessentially, in the form of Mustang. Arch-rival, General Motors replied with its Chevrolet Camaro, within the same year, and both the marquees became iconic & legendary and have been thriving even to this day, even more than half a century later, with their generational successors. Additionally, the VW Beetle became a symbol of the hippie counterculture of the 1960s and became highly popular as well as best-selling imported car in the U.S. during the 1960s decade.

The Cold War had been 'raging' and was almost at its peak during the 1960s decade. However, the extremely powerful forces of competition provided effective propulsion for immense scientific progress over the course of the tumultuous decade, in form of, technological leapfrogging and numerous breakthroughs achieved by both sides in this relentless ideological tug-of-war for supremacy and one-upmanship contest. The development of the U.S.' next-generation of fighter jets, namely, the F-14 Tomcat for the U.S. Navy and the F-15 Eagle for the U.S. Air Force, also started in the late 1960s, following dogfight debacles experienced against the North Vietnamese & their Russian MiGs, during the Vietnam war.

On the commercial aviation front, the Europeans had been opening the frontiers of air travel, beyond the sub-sonic part of the spectrum, in the very same decade and were gearing up to build the world's first supersonic passenger airliner, the Concorde, which was launched in 1962 and was the highlight of the decade for Europe in the commercial aviation space. On the other side of the Atlantic, the launch of Boeing's 747 in the United States was the tipping point for commercial aviation in the late 1960s. In fact, the Americans had also launched their own Supersonic Transport (SST), within a year of Concorde's launch, aimed at countering & allaying the fears of a potential European monopoly of the supersonic commercial airliner market going forward. However, the SST ultimately was scrapped owing to the oil crisis.

Space frontiers had already been forced open by the fierce competitive intensity at play, between America & the Soviet Union, with the Soviets having fired the unanticipated opening salvo, with the launch of the Sputnik in 1957, thereby, laying the foundations for and effectively launching the space war for manned space conquests in the 1960s. The 'Sputnik' moment had effectively shocked entire America as well as the Western World and, thus, made JFK vying for the moon by the end of the 1960s decade.

The race for space supremacy, ultimately, was won comprehensively by the United States with the victory (spearheaded by the development of the space shuttle program by the end of the 60s decade) realized, in form, of the successful Apollo-11 moon landings in 1969 which provided a grand finish to an incredible decade with an indelible U.S. stamp of technological authority getting duly & firmly established at the global stage.

On the military aviation front, the United States already had its U2 spy plane in the 1950s capable of flying undetected at altitudes of almost 70,000 feet, courtesy, the engineering genius of Kelly Johnson & Skunk Works. The U2 followed Kelly's earlier exploration of the gospels of high-altitude flying with Wiley Post which had provided the barebones & skeletal outline for his further MacGyvering and engineering brilliance. Wiley Post, in fact, had pioneered & mastered many tenets of high-altitude flying having conducted multiple in-flight experiments with his rudimentary gear and scant resources, in turn, also becoming the first & fastest pilot to fly solo around the world in 8 days setting a new world record way back in 1931.

The development & limitations of the U2 program effectively paved the way for the creation of Kelly's magnum opus, the SR-71 Blackbird, the fastest air-breathing manned aircraft ever built by mankind capable of flying at Mach 3+, which had its first flight in 1964 and entered service during the same decade, two years later in 1966. The SR-71's unique propulsion system, the revolutionary Pratt & Whitney J58 engine along with its variable air intake system, also earned a Collier Trophy to its designer, Skunk Works' Ben Rich (for the air intake system). The J58, developed by Pratt & Whitney for the CIA's A-12, USAF's SR-71 Blackbird & the Lockheed's YF-12 aircraft programs, brought in a number of technological breakthroughs which enabled significant technological leapfrogging on the military as well as commercial aviation fronts over the subsequent years.

These technological breakthroughs, especially on the military aviation side, spearheaded by the J58 engine program & other military turbojets developed by both GE Aviation & Pratt & Whitney; found their way into commercial aviation as well and spurred the development of new engine programs for commercial aviation, which essentially were derived from their military counterparts.

Pratt & Whitney, as the early market mover, developed the JT3D & JT8D, as its early, low bypass engines to power narrow bodies in the late 1950s & early 1960s, derived from its J57 & J52 military turbojets. The JT9D turbofan engine was subsequently developed by Pratt & Whitney engineers in the mid-1960s for powering the Boeing's latest aircraft program. GE Aviation also developed its iconic CF6 turbofan engine in the late 1960s, which continues to be in service and production, even today in the year 2023.

The JT9D was the first high-bypass ratio turbofan engine built for wide body aircrafts in commercial aviation by Pratt & Whitney, with the engine run for the first time in December 1966, a seminal year of sorts for commercial aviation as it went on to witness the creation of the aircraft, which actually revolutionized commercial aviation. It also quietly ushered in the era, which was to be ruled by the 'Queen of the Skies', the Boeing 747, which was to change the landscape of commercial aviation fundamentally & forever, in the truly rebellious spirit of the 1960s...

Chapter III

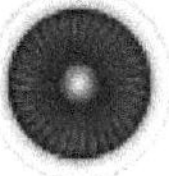

The 'Early' Power Plays

The Dawn of Jet Age and the Early, Low-Bypass Turbofans

Commercial aviation had already taken off with the dawn of the jet age, first in Europe in the early 1950s and later in America in the late 1950s, spearheaded largely by the Boeing's 707 program in the U.S., which had (since its launch in 1957) by then positioned itself superbly as the leading market player along with its smaller variant, the 720, with the competing Douglas DC-8, powered by Pratt & Whitney's JT3C turbojets, trailing far behind. The 707, however, was a narrow body aircraft and the surge in passenger traffic during the 1960s had already started choking & causing congestion at the airports, as serving burgeoning passenger traffic with narrow bodies meant frequent flights and an overwhelmed aviation infrastructure, which created another market opportunity which was duly seized and capitalized upon by Boeing in the 1960s with the world's first wide body aircraft program, the 747.

Turbofans vs. Turbojets – The Evolutionary Perspective

Turbofans were a natural, evolutionary extension of the turbojets, with the endeavor undertaken right after the end of World War II by the British engineers. Structurally, the difference between the turbojets and turbofans lies in their operating mechanisms led by the overall passage of the air through the engine core. In turbojets, all of the inlet air passes through the combustion chamber & the turbines directly while in the turbofans some of the inlet air goes into the combustion chamber & turbine (engine core) while some of it bypasses them with the use of a ducted fan.

Thus, the turbofan essentially is a turbojet mated to a ducted fan with both of these contributing to generation of thrust and the ratio of air going into the core vs. the air bypassing the core (termed bypass ratio) determining the thrust & fuel efficiency of the engine. The civilian turbofans used in commercial aviation have a majority of the air bypassing the core as they essentially need maximum fuel efficiency while powering commercial airliners & ferrying passengers while in military turbofans a majority of the air goes into the core rather than bypassing it to generate maximum thrust which the military aircrafts need for performance.

Further, commercial turbofans are designed for efficiency, reliability and durability given the fact that commercial airliners almost clock 3,000 to 4,000 flight hours per year while military turbofans are designed for maximum performance & reliability and fighter jets clock these many flight hours over their entire lifespan of around 3 to 4 decades.

The early turbofans were developed by the industry to address two key problems with the turbojets. First was their low fuel efficiency and the second was high noise. The turbojets had poor thermodynamic efficiency due to a low pressure ratio which was later addressed with improved materials & changes in compressor designs. The turbojets also had poor propulsive efficiency due to a high specific thrust/high velocity exhaust which is more suitable for supersonic stages of the flight.

For this reason, turbojets are still used in missiles & some UAVs, which more or less fly mostly at supersonic speeds throughout their flight trajectories while the civilian turbofans, with their high bypass ratios, are mostly used in commercial aviation for flying at high sub-sonic speeds to generate maximum fuel efficiencies.

The early, low bypass turbofans had a multi-stage fan behind the inlet guide vanes which produced a relatively high pressure ratio as compared to turbojets. Thus, in the original, low-bypass turbofans the propulsive efficiency was somewhat improved by reducing the exhaust velocity as compared to the turbojets. However, their bypass ratios were still low and almost the same as their military counterparts used in fighter jets.

For instance, the world's first production turbofan engine, Conway from Rolls Royce was introduced in the late 1950s, featuring a very low bypass ratio of 0.3 which was essentially the same as the GE's F404 military turbofan engine developed in the 1970s and which powers the Boeing's F/A-18 Hornet and was also used on the world's first stealth fighter, the F-117 Nighthawk built by Lockheed Corporation. For this reason of low-bypass ratio, the Conway was extremely noisy (especially during take-offs) despite the incorporation of mechanical noise suppression mechanisms (hush kits) and had relatively very little fuel efficiency improvements over turbojets of just 2% and was, thus, had a relatively very short life span in which it powered the early variants of Boeing's 707 (707-420) & DC-8 (DC-8-40) in late 1950s & early 1960s.

Pratt & Whitney vs. Rolls Royce in the Late 1950s

Pratt & Whitney was aware of the competition & the looming threat from Rolls Royce's Conway and developed its JT3D low-bypass turbofan engine in the early 1960s for the 707 & DC-8, which were originally powered by the Pratt & Whitney's JT3C & JT4A turbojets. The JT3D was, in fact, Pratt & Whitney's first commercial production turbofan and was, in turn, derived from its J57/JT3C turbojet developed in the early 1950s, primarily for military applications, as the practice of deriving engine variants for commercial applications from military engines has been common & rampant among engine OEMs throughout the history of aviation.

The J57-derived JT3D (USAF designation TF33) powered the original B-52H Stratofortress Bomber program in the mid-1950s along with the E-3 Sentry AWACS, KC-135 & E-8 JSTARS aircraft programs. The JT3D had a 2-stage fan set-up and had a bypass ratio of 1.42:1 along with an overall pressure ratio of 16:1 while generating a max thrust output of 17,000 lbf. The JT3D turned out to be one of the very successful engine programs for Pratt & Whitney with around 8,000 engines produced over the 1959 to 1985 period while the in-service fleets of around 1,000 TF33 engines-powered B-52 & E3 AWACS aircrafts, some of which are still in service, have collectively accumulated over 72 million flight hours over the past 6 decades[3].

Pratt & Whitney even provided the operators of early variants of 707/720s & DC-8s, powered by its JT3C turbojets, with conversion kits which could convert them effectively to the JT3D standard during shop visits leading to a 35% increase in thrust output along with a 15% to 22% improvement in fuel efficiency along with a reduction in noise output of almost 10 decibels without adding any weight penalty[4]. That's how Pratt & Whitney effectively torpedoed Rolls Royce's Conway and its market prospects.

Pratt & Whitney even developed another low-bypass turbofan engine in the early 1960s which was designated as the JT8D. The JT8D was derived from Pratt & Whitney's J52 turbojet engine, which had powered the U.S. Navy's A-6 Intruder and A-4 Skyhawk attack aircrafts and had in fact been developed itself from the J57. The JT8D had a thrust output range of 12,250 lbf to 17,400 lbf with a bypass ratio of 0.96:1. It was developed for & ultimately debuted on the Boeing's 727, earliest members of the 737 program (737-100 & 737-200) and the DC-9.

The Coup by Pratt & Whitney Engineers

There is a very interesting, real story behind how Pratt & Whitney engineers, as described by author Jack Connors, a Pratt & Whitney engineer, in his book, "Engines of Pratt & Whitney – A Technical History"[6], effectively staged a coup to ultimately get Pratt & Whitney on to the Boeing's 727 program which was all set to be powered by Rolls Royce's Spey engines. Boeing was set to launch its 727 tri-jet program in the early 1960s to complement the 707 in its aircraft line-up and had already chosen the Rolls Royce's Spey engines to power it which were being heavily promoted by Rolls Royce at the time. United and Eastern Airlines were Boeing's potential launch customers for the 727 which were actively urging Pratt & Whitney to come up with a turbofan engine of its own or else they were "willing to go with the Rolls Royce engine!"[6]

Pratt & Whitney vs. Rolls Royce – Early Powerplays - Implications

Pratt & Whitney engineers got in touch with the technical personnel at Eastern & United Airlines, roped in their own top management and ultimately got the green light for the proposal to develop the JT8D from the J52 turbojet internally with full backing and development funding. The development started in the 1960 and the JT8D engine was ultimately born in the 1963.

The development, however, had major implications for both Pratt & Whitney and for Rolls Royce. The development of the JT8D and getting onboard the 727 program, which was one of the most successful commercial aircraft programs of the 1960s, gave Pratt & Whitney a virtual head start in the commercial aircraft market with a relatively reliable & maintenance friendly low-bypass turbofan which went on to dominate the narrow body aircraft market for almost next two decades while effectively keeping Rolls Royce out of it once again.

For Rolls Royce, the 727 would have been the perfect timing & opportunity to foray into the commercial aviation market for a long haul but Pratt & Whitney's engineers ensured that it did not happen! Just the way they had denied Rolls Royce (with its Conway & Avon turbojets) earlier with the development of JT3Ds for DC-8 & 707 quad jets. Further, across the North Atlantic in Europe, Rolls' own backyard, the JT8D ultimately powered the later variants of French Dassault Mercure and the Super Caravelle B aircraft programs as well.

Pratt & Whitney, later in the 1970s, also developed the JT8D-200 variant featuring a higher thrust output range of 18,500 to 21,700 lbf along with a higher bypass ratio of 1.74:1 which ultimately powered the McDonnell Douglas' MD-80 program. A total of around 14,750 JT8D engines were produced by Pratt & Whitney of which around 20% or 2,900 engines were the -200 variants and the JT8D engines remained the industry benchmark for reliability for almost 2+ decades till the advent & market domination of CFM56.

Pratt & Whitney vs. GE in the 1960s

Pratt & Whitney, thus, was a dominant industry force when it came to aircraft propulsion in the 1960s given its strong market positioning & well-established presence in the military aircraft propulsion market with the J52, J57, TF33 & the J58/JT11 engine (and their derivatives) and well-entrenched presence on some of the most important, highly successful & almost iconic military aircraft programs in the USAF's force structure, namely, the B-52 Bomber, KC-135 aerial tanker, the SR-71 Blackbird, E-3 Sentry AWACS & E-8 JSTARS and the C-141 Starlifter with many of these still around almost over more than half a century later.

In commercial aviation, engines derived from the J57 powered almost all of the leading aircraft programs developed by Boeing & McDonnell Aircraft, namely,

707, 727, 737-100 & -200, DC-9 & later the MD-80. Pratt & Whitney, thus, produced around 22,000+ engines (including those derived from) based on its J57 platform for military & commercial usage from 1950s to almost 1980s. Pratt & Whitney was also the pioneer in developing the industry's first production afterburning turbofan engine, in form of the TF-30 in 1964, which powered the General Dynamics' F-111, Northrop's F-14A Tomcat and the A-7 Corsair II with a non-afterburning variant.

The other major industry force & aviation powerhouse competing head-to-head with Pratt & Whitney in the military aircraft propulsion market during the 1950s & 1960s, undoubtedly, was General Electric. GE Aviation, with its J79 & J85 turbojet engine programs, was truly was a strong market force and leader, especially, in the fighter jet propulsion market. In fact, Pratt & Whitney had the J57 as the bedrock of its engines line-up while GE had J79 as the core of its engines portfolio.

The J79 powered the McDonnell Douglas' F-4 Phantom II interceptor & fighter-bomber as the sole powerplant which was the backbone of the fighting capabilities of the U.S. Navy, USMC & later the U.S. Air Force from the late 1950s to the 1960s. Other key military aircraft programs powered by the J79, included, the Convair B-58 Hustler, Lockheed's F-104 Starfighter and the North American A-5 Vigilante.

GE's J85 engine, derived from the J79 as its smaller sibling, powered the U.S. Navy's F-5 Tiger fighter jet platform developed by Northrop Corporation (which entered service in the early 1960s) along with the T-38 Talon trainer aircraft which entered service with the USAF in the early 1960s and is still very much out there even almost 6+ decades later now awaiting Boeing's T-7A Red Hawk to get fully airborne.

It would be important to note here that Pratt & Whitney's stronghold clearly was large military aircrafts which needed multiple engines to power them while GE's forte was fighter jets needing a pair of turbofans at the most. The B-52H, for instance, had 8 TF33-P-3/103 turbofan engines powering it with each engine producing 17,000 lbf of thrust output. On the contrary, GE mostly powered fighter jets during this era which had a maximum of two engines powering them. This is what created the disparity in the cumulative number of engines produced by Pratt & Whitney and GE during this phase with Pratt & Whitney having produced 22,000+ J57 engines while GE produced around 17,000+ J79 engines.

Secondly, fighter jets of the 1960s era were relatively short lived with a limited lifespan as the technology, competition and threats evolved rapidly and their capability limitations vis-à-vis Russian fighters during the Vietnam War. It led to their production lines getting wound up by the 1980s and the next generation fighters taking over as early as the 1970s, led by, the F-14 Tomcat, F-15 Eagle and the F-16 Fighting Falcon.

On the contrary, large bombers & commercially-derived support aircrafts, like the B-52H, KC-135, E-3 & the E-8, have relatively had a very long lifespan and are still around in the 21st century and are now being recapitalized gradually. For instance, the re-engining of the B-52H was initiated by the USAF in 2021 and the fleet is going to be in-service at least till the middle of the current century. This has proved to be advantageous for Pratt & Whitney, in terms, of the incoming revenue streams from the MRO activity and systems upgrades.

However, on the commercial side of the aviation market, GE relatively had very limited inroads with the company having developed a civilian version of its J79 engine platform, the CJ805, which was available in two variants, namely, CJ805-3 & the CJ805-23 with the former one being a turbojet and the latter being a turbofan generating a thrust output of around 16,000 lbf.

The CJ805-3 powered around 65 Convair 880s while the CJ805-23 was used on the Convair 990 airliners of which only 37 were built. GE also developed the much smaller, aft-fan based CF700 turbofan engine for business aviation application with a thrust output of 4,500 lbf, derived from the CJ610 turbojet, which ultimately powered the Dassault Falcon 20 and the North American Sabreliner business jets in the mid-1960s. Both Falcon 20 & the Sabreliner proved to be quite popular with around 500+ units of the Falcon 20 manufactured by Dassault (with around a third going to Pan Am's business jets division) while around 800+ Sabreliners were produced by North American.

Thus, on a comparative basis, GE was almost a fringe player in the commercial aviation market in the 1960s, as compared to Pratt & Whitney, which was almost a powerhouse as well as a behemoth with engines produced by Pratt & Whitney powering almost 90% of the commercial airplanes in the 1950s & 1960s. However, on the military side of the market, both were almost equals, in terms, of technology, capabilities and market presence, as well as positioning, with both well-entrenched in their respective niches & segments.

Rolls Royce and the 1960s Decade

It would also be important at this stage to look at what Rolls Royce had been up to during this period after having launched the Conway in the 1950s as the world's first low bypass turbofan engine. Conway effectively powered the Handley Page Victor, Vickers VC10 and the early versions of Boeing 707-420 and the Douglas DC-8-40 before being effectively sidelined by the Pratt & Whitney's JT3D with the 797 & DC-8 switching to the JT3D given it's relatively much higher bypass ratio and lower noise profile than Conway.

Conway, with its 17,500 lbf thrust output, was targeted at what at the time was the top end of the market and was too large for the smaller aircrafts being developed at the time, namely, Sud Caravelle, BAC One-Eleven and the Hawker Siddeley Trident which would have needed a smaller engine. Rolls Royce, thus, shifted its focus on to a relatively smaller turbofan engine, designated Spey, after Rolls Royce's traditional convention of naming its engines after rivers in the United Kingdom.

Spey, with a max thrust output of 12,100 lbf. (dry mode on Spey Mk 202) and a bypass ratio of 0.64:1, entered service in 1964 powering the BAC 1-11 and the Hawker Siddeley Trident with further variants of Spey, featuring higher power ratings, introduced through the 1960s decade. The Spey went on to power the Blackburn Buccaneer, based on a militarized variant of the Spey powering the BAC 1-11, and also powered the Fokker F-28 Fellowship.

Spey was also used as the sole powerplant for the British variant of the McDonnell Douglas' F-4 Phantom II, designated Phantom FG.Mk.1 and FGR.Mk.2, with the Spey replacing GE's J79 turbojets used on the Phantom

IIs operated by the U.S. The Spey 201 turbofans, with their 20,515 lbf thrust (wet mode), were almost 25% more powerful than the J79 turbojets (given their 16,000 lbf thrust output in wet mode) which provided a 10% improvement in combat radius and a 15% better ferry range on the British Phantoms while also enabling operations from smaller aircraft carriers operated by the Royal Navy with additional take-off thrust generated by the higher-rated Spey engines.

Another variant of Spey was developed jointly by Rolls Royce & Allison for the U.S. market, designated as the TF41 with a thrust output of 14,250 lbf and a bypass ratio of 0.77:1, with Allison ultimately producing the TF41 in the U.S. under a license from Rolls Royce. The TF41 powered the USAF's LTV A-7D Corsair and the U.S. Navy's A-7E from 1968-1983 with a total of 1,440 TF41s produced by Allison. Another variant of Spey, the Spey 807, also powered the AMX International AMX, the joint attack aircraft program jointly developed by Italy and Brazil in the 1980s, with around 200 aircrafts produced.

Overall, a total of around 2,800 Spey engines were built by Rolls Royce, with their relatively much lower maintenance costs & high engine reliability, ensuring a long in-service utilization for them despite the emergence of newer turbofan engines in the 1970s, featuring relatively much higher bypass ratios & fuel efficiencies, with the aviation versions of the base model of Spey alone having accumulated over 50 million[5] flight hours over 30+ years of utilization, as per Rolls Royce[1].

The Age of High-Bypass Turbofans

Commercial aviation had already taken off on to the flight path charting the next phase of its growth trajectory following the dawn of the jet age in the 1950s, spearheaded largely by the Boeing's 707 in North America, which had (since its launch in 1957) by then positioned itself superbly as the market leader & its mainstay, along with its smaller variant, the 720, with the Douglas DC-8 trailing way behind. The 707, however, was a narrow body and the surge in passenger traffic during the 1960s had already led to choking & congestion

---

1. https://www.rolls-royce.com/products-and-services/defence/aerospace/combat-jets/spey.aspx

at airports as serving burgeoning passenger traffic with narrow bodies meant frequent flights and an overwhelmed aviation infrastructure.

Pratt & Whitney, with its first high bypass JT9D turbofan engine, effectively unlocked & heralded a new era in commercial aviation which was about very large, wide body aircrafts which were truly the zeitgeist of the times as they were required to ferry passengers in bulk, in order, to decongest the airports and other limited aviation infrastructure of the era, in terms of relative size & scale. A perfect example of it was the Boeing's 737 program designed in the 1960s, featuring a low ground clearance, intended at matching the aviation infrastructure of the time with the low ingress & egress enabling faster deplaning & boarding of the aircrafts by the passengers.

The advent of the JT9D engine on the horizon had, thus, effectively unlocked an irresistible proposition & the next level of the aerial contest among airlines as well as the aircraft OEMs, which was all about developing & deploying larger, wider aircrafts with more than one aisle to accommodate a large number of passengers in a single flight.

This was truly aligned with the traditional, long standing convention in commercial aviation with technological evolution & generational leaps in engine technology driving development of new airplanes by the industry. The JT9D, thus, was the watershed moment in commercial aviation as it acted as the much needed catalyst in shaping the future of commercial aviation from hereupon by catalyzing the genesis of wide body aircrafts with the idea's journey from inception to materialization just being a matter of time.

There, however, was another factor at play in the background from the supply side and it was the USAF's search for a strategic airlifter just prior to the onset of the Vietnam War as the service had been in the process of transitioning from the era of the propeller powered transport aircrafts to jet aircrafts.

Genesis of 747 and the JT9D

The USAF needed a very large military transport aircraft for logistics operations, in order, to be able to transport oversize cargo & equipment across all parts of the globe to support its force projection capabilities. The USAF had, thus, outlined requirements & floated the RFP for the CX-Heavy Logistics System (CX-HLS) program in early 1964.

As per the RFP, the aircraft needed to be a quadjet with an 81 tons airlift capacity (similar to the C-17 Globemaster III which was to be procured by the USAF two decades later in the 1980s) in a huge cargo bay, which had to be designed precisely to the Air Force specifications and had to be accessible by doors from the front as well as rear for ease of loading & offloading oversize cargo.

The CX-HLS was to supplement another cargo aircraft, the Lockheed built C-141 Starlifter, which was being inducted by the USAF in the mid-1960s, to replace its older propeller powered airlifters which had served the service well but were technologically obsolete and were falling short, in terms of capabilities, in the jet age.

Boeing, Douglas & Lockheed were the triad of shortlisted airframers, which had made the cut, while Pratt & Whitney and GE had been picked up by the USAF for engines. The final contract award, however, went to Lockheed Corporation which went on to create the C-5 Galaxy while GE made a crucial win on the powerplant front with its TF-39 engine, which locked horns with the Pratt & Whitney's proposed JTF14 engine, developed specifically for the C-5 program featuring cutting edge technologies & significant advances in material sciences.

The TF-39 engine (and its subsequent transformation as the venerable CF6) was going to play a pivotal role in GE's journey going forward in its bid to ultimately usurp the Pratt & Whitney dynasty in the commercial aviation market. Coming to Boeing, it did lose the program but the proposal and the design it had fielded was going to have momentous implications for commercial aviation going forward.

Juan Trippe, Founder & President of Pan Am, had already sown the seed for the creation of world's first wide body aircraft by having requested Boeing in the early 1960s for an aircraft more than twice the size of the existing 707 to accommodate rapidly growing passenger air traffic (which had grown almost at 15%[7] annually for 1965 & 1966), as forecasted by industry watchers as well as the FAA, who were anticipating a further surge in air traffic for the 1970s decade which would have justified the development of a much larger airplane to carry passengers in bulk and to decongest airports.

Further, following Lockheed's win on the C-5 Galaxy program, Boeing & Douglas, the reigning commercial aviation giants, were insecure that Lockheed could derive & carve a commercial derivative out of the C-5 which could effectively threaten their respective market shares. In this regard, somehow, they were spot-on as Lockheed could not resist the idea & ultimately went on to creating the L-1011 trijet.

Juan Trippe contacted the losing team on the C-5 program, Boeing and Pratt & Whitney, as they had the technology building blocks ready, for the creation of 747. He also placed an initial, launch order for 747s in April 1966 by arranging special financing and he is, therefore, duly considered by the industry as the father of the 747, in addition, to Boeing's Joe Sutter, the actual designer of the 747. Boeing had also been working on the development of the 737 in the mid-1960s with Lufthansa scrupulously controlling & shaping the same as the launch customer of 737 with Boeing airplane designers, Jack Steiner and Joe Sutter, actively engaged in fleshing out the 737.

Following the loss on the USAF's C-5 program and with Pan Am getting onboard by firmly placing the order for 747 as the launch customer, Boeing teamed up with Pratt & Whitney as the engine provider and launched the 747 program with an ambitious timeline for the roll out of the 747 set for fall of 1969 with Pan Am aggressively pushing for the same. Joe Sutter, thus, was moved from the 737 & deployed on to the 747 program by 1965

Pan Am had already placed the order for 25 Boeing 747s in April 1966, worth over $500 million, thereby, becoming the launch customer and, thus, effectively laying the foundation for the creation of the world's first wide body aircraft. It was a move, which was in-line and aligned with the company's own longstanding tradition, of accelerating & shaping the industry's technological evolution. The 747 was to be powered by the Pratt & Whitney's high bypass

JT9D turbofan engines, thereby, marking a key departure from the prevailing generation of low bypass turbofan engines.

Boeing proudly displayed the 747 at the Paris Air Show held in 1969, sharing the limelight with the highly touted Concorde, which too, had Pan Am as one of its key launch customers, truly marking a giant leap forward into the future for commercial aviation...

Chapter IV

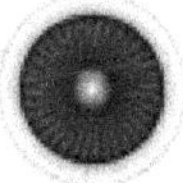

The Coronation of the 'Queen'

"The Second phase of the jet age – the era of the jumbo transport and the truly mass airlift – is irrevocably here. But many of the gigantic economic problems that attended the premature birth of this graceful flying whale have not been resolved"[Z]. That's how a New York Times article titled 'Giant Jets Pose Giant Problems' published on April 09, 1972 described & summarized as to how the commercial aviation landscape had been impacted & transformed by the advent of the Boeing's 747 which was also being referred to as 'Tragicomedy'[Z] in the business circles. The reason for that were Boeing's overpromises on the 747 program and its relative under-delivery and coming short on many of them, especially, on the operating economics front.

For instance, Boeing had promised a 30% to 35%[Z] savings in operating costs given that the 747 was almost two-and-a-half times the size of a 707 which would have led to realization of cost savings emanating from the economies of scale. This logic, given by Boeing, actually accelerated the airlines' transition from 707s & DC-8s towards the way larger 747.

However, in reality, that number came down only by 17% to 19%[Z] as reported by Pan Am and American Airlines. Additionally, the flying public was sold the dream of low flying fares on the very same premise of economies of scale which were to be provided by the 747 program. But in reality it did not materialize owing to the higher than promised maintenance costs on the 747, which as per Pan Am, were almost double the maintenance costs of the older 707s.

The advent of the 747 was, thus, the fulfillment of a dream, a generational shift technologically and a set of shattered promises, all at the very same time, from the perspective of the flying public, industry, operating airlines & the stakeholders. Let's explore the technological shift aspect from the propulsion system's perspective.

JT9D: A Leap into the Future

The JT9D engine, which was developed to power the 747, was derived from the STF200/JTF14 demonstrator program developed by Pratt & Whitney to power the USAF's proposed C-5 heavy airlifter. Pratt & Whitney; knowing that a higher thrust, next generation engine would be required for the C-5; started the detailed design phase of the STF200 program in early 1963 aimed at the 31,000-lb thrust class with a pressure ratio of around 20:1 and a bypass ratio of 2:1[6].

The JTF14 was the ultimate derivative of the STF200 program with the ultimate thrust output of 41,000 lbf and a bypass ratio of 3.5:1[6] and this was the specific engine variant which had been proposed by Pratt & Whitney to the USAF for the C-5 program. The STF200/JTF-14, thus, was Pratt & Whitney's second-generation turbofan engine with the earlier JT3D, JT8D & the TF33 being the first generation turbofans.

The primary difference between the JT3D and the JTF14 was the overall design modification along with simplification & compaction of overall engine architecture, in addition, to a significant increase in pressure ratio which had gone up from 12:1 (for the earlier variants of JT3D and 16:1 for the JT3D-8A) to almost 20:1[6] on the JTF14 indicating a substantial increase in thermal efficiency. The bypass ratio on the JTF14, too, had gone up to 3.5:1 as compared to 1.42:1 on the JT3D while the thrust had increased by almost 2.5 times from 17,000 lbf (for the JT3D) to 41,000 lbf (on the JTF14).

The JT9D engine was formally launched by Pratt & Whitney in 1965 with the JT9D-3 being the first certified engine variant producing 43,500 lbf[6] of thrust. The primary reason as to why the development of the JT9D was truly a generational leap into the future for the industry emanates from an almost 2-fold increase in the thrust output it provided (with the generation of 43,500 lbf of thrust output for the JT9D-3A which was to power the 747-100, the initial version of the 747, launched in 1966) as compared to the maximum 22,500 lbf of thrust generated by the largest variant of the JT3D, the JT3D-15, which was to power the Boeing 707-820. Additionally, the significant increase in bypass ratio achieved on the JT9D, up from 1.42:1 on the JT3D to almost

4.8:1 on the JT9D-7R4 variant which entered service in late 1980, was also significant from a technology evolution perspective.

Secondly, the utilization of advances in material science innovations, especially, the utilization of Nickel & Titanium alloys in the hot sections for improved thermal efficiency & reliability apart from incorporation of advanced technologies in structures & aerodynamics. However, the timeline under which the entire 747 program was to be developed could easily be termed as highly ambitious given that it needed almost a quantum leap in technology without the luxury of requisite time required to test & mature next-generation technologies, especially, on the engine front, which ultimately & invariably led to troubles, delays & teething troubles even long after the 747's formal entry into service.

Another challenging aspects of the JT9D engine's commercialization for Pratt & Whitney was the development of a new engine case design, which was to incorporate a much larger front mounted fan with a diameter of 92.3 inches/ 2.34 meters (for initial variants) for producing a high-bypass ratio of almost 5:1, unlike any previous commercial engines developed by Pratt & Whitney, which had a max bypass ratio of 1.4:1 (on the JT3D-1).

The fan on the JT9D engine almost had a 75% larger diameter of 2.34 meter as against 1.35 meter on the JT3D-1. Such a large fan needed a completely new engine casing design capable of withstanding such a high bypass ratio and thrust output. Engine casings on all previous, first generation Pratt & Whitney turbofans had been simple, cylindrical & tube-like in design. However, the JT9D needed a new casing with a radically different design geometry which had to be designed from scratch while racing against time in order to meet the ambitious development schedule of the 747.

An article, published in March 2011, by former Pratt & Whitney employee, Lee S. Langston, who was directly involved in the development of the JT9D engine as a young engineer in the 1960s, delved much deeper into the issue and provides an excellent analysis of the same.

He further elaborates in his article, "Pratt & Whitney engineers came up with a case shaped like a fat-stemmed sunflower. The front fan and its surrounding fan case duct constituted the sunflower and the rest of the jet engine case was the stem"[8]. However, the case would subsequently experience a distortion of shape, from circular to elliptical, due to the bending effect created by high-thrust loading during take-offs leading to compressor & turbine blades physically rubbing against the casing's interior resulting in a reduction of overall thrust, along with an increase in fuel consumption, apart from causing structural damage to the casing interior.

The 747's flight test program, following the 747's maiden flight in February 1969, was hampered by this ovalization problem, in addition, to engine stalls which were being encountered routinely following rapid throttle movements, which collectively & effectively, delayed customer deliveries of the 747s by a month to January 1970 after the receipt of FAA certification in December 1969.

Two other factors also contributed to this ovalization problem, as per Lee, with the first one being the mounting of the JT9D engines by Boeing further forward on the leading edges of the wing to reduce drag & potential wing flutter problems.

The second one was a departure from the conventional way of mounting the JT9D engines under the 747's wing pylons which were to use turbine case-based mounting rather than the traditional practice of the usage of intermediate case mounts, which would have reduced weight and saved space. Both these factors directly led to ovalization of JT9D's engine casing upon take-off with the problem experienced even 6-months after the 747's entry into service.

An article appearing in the Times magazine in 1969 described the impact of the ovalization problem on Boeing and its airline customers in vivid details. The following excerpt from it captures the prevailing dynamic effectively, "On the apron outside Boeing's plant in Everett, Wash., 15 enormous 747 jets stand high and silent, harbingers of a new era in aviation. They are painted in the colors of several international airlines: TWA, Pan Am, Lufthansa, Air France.

For the moment, however, the planes are the world's largest gliders —because they have no engines. Pan Am had been scheduled to get the first three commercial giants, each with a capacity of 362 passengers, in late November. Last week, embarrassed Boeing officials said that performance difficulties in the Pratt & Whitney JT9D engines would delay that delivery by as much as eight weeks."[8]

Pratt & Whitney, which was a business division of United Aircraft back then, booked a charge of $137 million, attributed primarily, to the JT9D engine leading to a $43 million[7] net loss being booked by the United Aircraft Corporation for the year 1971, almost two years after the 747's (designated by Boeing as the 747-100) maiden flight on February 09, 1969, which too, incidentally, was delayed owing to engine overheating problem, even prior to the 747's take-off roll. In fact, even Boeing had instituted a $94 million[7] claim against United Aircraft over the JT9D's performance shortcomings.

The problem was deemed as a structural issue by Pratt & Whitney engineers and was ultimately traced to the position of the main thrust mount on the turbine case and was ultimately resolved by redesigning the thrust mount, following the usage of a Y-shaped, two-point thrust mount, for transferring thrust to the airframe.

The solution proved to be effective and was going to be almost epochal for commercial aviation given that the two-point mount design was subsequently used for mounting the GE90 and Trent 800 engines as well on the Boeing's 777[8] aircraft program in the early 1990s. The undisputed 'Queen of the Skies' was, thus, on her way to dominate the skies for decades to come as the world's first & largest wide body aircraft...

The 747, thus, had effectively heralded & unleashed the commercial aviation's second jet age, at the turn of the 1960s decade, propelled by the introduction of large, wide body aircrafts powered by high bypass turbofan engines with the industry eager for new equipment as well as technologies to meet surging air traffic growth rates.

Their euphoria, however, was going to be short lived as a major turbulence awaited them at the very start of the 1970s decade...

Chapter V

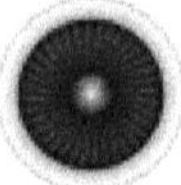

The 'Unprecedented' Turbulence

Pan Am's ambition & patronage of innovations, Boeing's $2 billion gamble and Pratt & Whitney's ingenuity & macgyvering, had collectively unleashed the era of wide bodies powered by the second generation of turbofans towards the end of the 1960s, following the certification of the 747 by the FAA in December 1969. Following the launch customer, Pan Am, many other airlines also ordered the 747 to maintain market parity, even when many of them did not even require the huge capacity provided by the 747 and they did so, evidently, purely for competitive reasons.

Pan Am's launch order for 25 initial 747s was followed by subsequent orders from international carriers, including, Lufthansa, Air France, Japan Airlines, BOAC & T.W.A. for the next 27 747s with American, Continental, Northwest & United soon joining the fray as the 747 frenzy was at its peak and none of the leading airlines wanted to miss out on it for prestige reasons. Former American Airlines President George Warde, who was at the helm of affairs from 1971-1974, recalled (regarding 747 order by American) & captured the prevailing market sentiment in a nutshell in an interview given by him to the New York Times decades ago, "We had to be competitive with T.W.A., which had to have it because Pan Am ordered it."[Z]

The 747 euphoria, however, was going to be a short lived phenomenon as nobody was paying heed to the brewing up of inflationary pressures, hidden underneath a strong economic showing, caused by rising fiscal spending on the Vietnam War and 'Great Society' programs being spearheaded by the President Lyndon B. Johnson's administration since 1965-1966, besides, the active pursuit of an easy monetary policy by the Fed to boost economic growth & employment.

The LBJ administration, however was, simultaneously, also making passive efforts, alongside, to contain inflationary pressures by cooling down the economy by exhorting businesses to put a cap on capital expenditures rather than directly raising interest rates. LBJ even tried to thwart the 747 program[Z], as part of his cooling down measures,but the persistence of Juan Trippe, ultimately won the day following his argument that the 747 would help address the Balance of Payment (BOP) problem, through exports to international carriers, while also enhancing America's technological leadership, which found favor even with the reigning Secretary of Defense, Robert McNamara.

The advent of the Richard Nixon administration to the White House in 1969 led to continued funding for the ongoing Vietnam War & increased social welfare spending (in view of the upcoming elections in 1971) while the objective of containing rising inflation levels was relegated to a secondary status, way down on the overall priority list. The focus, however, was instead on the pursuit of an easy monetary policy, characterized by low-interest rates, to promote growth & make the economy appear way stronger than it actually was, with the same spearheaded by Arthur Burns, the new Fed Chairman, who was appointed by the Nixon Administration in early 1970 to orchestrate it.

Nixon's subsequent decision to suspend gold convertibility of the U.S. Dollar in August 1971, led to a significant devaluation of the greenback, with a direct & significant impact on those exposed directly to the U.S. Dollar globally, especially, the Middle East- based oil producers, who lost substantial oil revenues, following the plummeting of the U.S. Dollar.

OPEC, which had already been established in the 1960s, started exercising active control over oil production & prices, following the U.S.' move and even retaliated by imposing an oil embargo on the U.S. in the 1973, intended at boosting oil prices and for punishing the U.S. administration for its support of Israel in the Yom Kippur War.

Nixon's re-election in 1972, following low-unemployment rates & strong economic growth numbers registered for 1972, was a major victory for the Republicans. However, imposition of wage & price controls, tax reform act and

the implementation of social security amendments, under H.R. 1[2], aimed at increased social welfare spending under Nixonomics, were enough to provide even more fuel to the inflationary flames, which had already been raging by now and ultimately reached double-digit levels. Nixon even was quoted as having said, "We'll take inflation if necessary, but we can't take unemployment."[10]

Inflation was prevailing at the 8.8% level in the year 1973, and fuelled further by the international oil crisis, had shot up to 12% by the end of the 1970s decade. By the start of the 1980s decade, inflation was surging at the 14% level and stood at 14.8% by March 1980. Paul Volcker, the incoming Fed Chair, who was appointed in early August 1979 under President Jimmy Carter, took the command of the battle to contain high inflation levels personally.

He had already been the under secretary of the Treasury for international monetary affairs, from 1969 to 1974, in the Nixon Administration. Under Volcker, the Fed aggressively pursued an unprecedented as well as painful tightening of the monetary policy with interest rates hiked to an almost unprecedented level of 20% in June 1981, up from an average of 11.2% in 1979.

The prime lending rate had also touched a high of 21.5% in 1981, causing a devastating impact on the economy, which rapidly contracted and precipitated a full-blown recession in the early 1980s with unemployment rates rising to over 10%. However, by the start of 1983, inflation had been fully crushed and the interest rates were back to the under 3% level.

The impact of such extreme volatility in macroeconomic conditions on commercial aviation, over the course of a decade, was tectonic in nature & far reaching in impact. The 747 had just taken off, with the start of customer deliveries in early 1970, while facing such massive headwinds & amid such unprecedented market turbulence. The domestic airline traffic grew by only 2% in 1971[7], as compared to almost 15% in the mid-1960s, while the North Atlantic traffic, too, registered only 4.6% growth.

However, by then, Boeing had already registered orders for around 210 aircrafts on the 747 program but Boeing could only book 7 new orders for the 747 for the year 1971. The production rate on the 747, too, was cut back drastically to only 2 aircrafts a month[7], despite a healthy order book.

Boeing, so far, had invested billions towards the development of the 747 and the establishment of a gigantic, new production facility, which had almost driven the company towards bankruptcy. However, Boeing had a narrow escape, as the company undertook significant cost cutting measures & initiated massive layoffs, while booking a miniscule profit for the year 1971.

The impact of macroeconomic turbulence on the airlines, however, was almost two-fold, given that an unprecedented surge in oil prices had already shot up their operating costs, while the spike in interest rates, had effectively ruined their fleet expansion & renewal plans, underscored by the acquisition of newer, more fuel efficient airplanes (as was being promised by Boeing with the 747).

Additionally, airline business typically is cyclical and is marked by alternating cycles of upswings & downswings, lasting almost 7-years, and driven, primarily, by the macroeconomic forces at play and it was the onset of one such cycle for the industry in the 1970s decade. The profitability of the airlines had been mostly in red, since the peak of 1966, wherein, the airline industry had registered record profits of $427.6 million[11] which was followed by the onset of a consistent, downward spiral.

The net profits for the U.S. Scheduled Airline Industry had plummeted by almost 75%, from $216.1 million[11] for the year 1968 to a mere 55.3 million[11] for 1969, a decline of almost 87% from the peak of 1966, as per the official publication of the Air Transport Association of America[11] for 1970, with operating expenses for airlines having risen way more (16%) than the revenues growth (13%). The report mentions explicitly, "Rapidly increasing costs in every phase of airline operations – labor, interest expense, landing fees and rentals at airports, fuels and supplies – have been the principal cause for the decline in the industry's earnings position."[11]

Domestic airlines, consequently, were allowed to increase fares across-the-board, by the Civil Aeronautics Board (CAB) in early 1969, as a measure to address the industry's deteriorating financial condition, which was expected to increase revenues by around 4%. However, it was offset effectively by rising inflation levels in less than half a year, as per the ATAA report. It was followed by restructuring of domestic fares by the CAB, based on a new pricing formula in late 1969, which was expected to lead to another 6% increase in revenues for airlines.

CAB's comments, following the restructuring of fares in late 1969, however, indicate that it was aware that the measures might prove to be inadequate, "In light of the low level of earnings realized in the most recent periods and the inflationary cost increases being experienced by the carriers, there appears to be no prospect that the fare increases approved herein will enable the industry to reach the 10.5% return guideline in the immediate future."[11]

Opening remarks from Stuart G Tipton, the reigning President of the Air Transport Association of America, in the 1970 edition of the report, provide a much clearer perspective on the prevailing industry sentiment, characterized by the significant investments scheduled towards recapitalization of equipment amid prevailing difficult market conditions and increased support expectations from the federal government in a highly regulated industry structure.

He mentions, "We are now in the beginning of the second jet age, one which is being characterized by the introduction of new wide-body jet aircraft, capable of carrying up to 450 passengers. And the commitment (from airlines) is larger than ever. All told, the airlines will invest $10 billion in capital expenditure for the period 1970 through 1973. Of this amount, $6.6 billion is for new aircraft alone – almost exclusively wide-bodied jet aircraft. This comes at a time when airline profits are alarmingly low and first quarter signs in 1970 indicate further deterioration."[11]

Almost, 11 of the 12 major U.S. airlines had been registering a rapid increase in overall losses with Pan Am alone having booked losses for four straight years from 1968 to 1971 after the retirement of Juan Trippe in 1968.

Amid such widespread market volatility and economic turmoil, the impact on airlines and on their operating expenses, of the upcoming oil crisis, which hit precisely in October 1973, would have been nothing short of catastrophic with the oil prices having risen by a third from an average of $2.96[12] for 1970 to $4.08[12] by 1973, which went further up by four-times to $12.52[12] by 1974, following the imposition of OPEC's oil embargo.

The market carnage and mayhem, however, did not stop here with oil prices maintaining their upward growth trajectory reaching $21.57[12] in 1979, following the break-out of the Iran-Iraq war, accompanied by the unprecedented tax rate increase by the Fed to 20%. Oil prices went further up to $33.86[12] by 1980, in the wake of the Iranian revolution, and by 1981, they were at an all-time high of $37.10[12], having started out from $2.96 in 1970, an almost twelve-fold plus increase recorded in just over a single decade's span...

Following the unprecedented surge in oil prices, a R&D effort was initiated under a NASA Aircraft Energy Efficiency aeronautical research program, with its genesis in 1975, aimed at potentially developing highly fuel efficient aircraft propulsion technology, designated as Prop Fans, for commercial aviation applications.

The propfan technology was intended at blending the higher speed & performance of traditional turbofans with the high fuel efficiency of conventional turboprops to take on the surge & the volatility in the global crude oil market. The aviation industry was avidly looking forward to the prospects of an almost 30% improvement in fuel efficiency being proposed by the prop fan technology over traditional turbofans.

The program led to the development of the GE36 experimental aircraft engine, simply known, as the Unducted Fan (UDF) or Propfan (more on that in Chapter 16), which was proposed for the Boeing's 7J7 and the McDonnell Douglas' MD-94X aircraft concepts during the mid-1980s but it could not see the light of the day due to plummeting of the oil prices in the 1980s.

However, the technology is making a comeback in a new avatar, in form of CFM International's (GE Aviation & Safran's engines JV) RISE program, which aims at a 20% increase in fuel efficiency and emission levels with a projected certification & commercial availability by 2035.

Boeing, 747 and the Economic Headwinds & Market Turmoil of the 1970s

The onset of economic turmoil & market volatility for airlines and a rapid increase in airfares impacted general public's interest in flying and Boeing's

Chapter VI

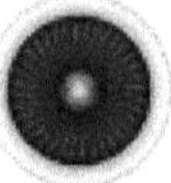

The Genesis of an 'Icon'

GE's Incredible Comeback to Commercial Aviation

The market landscape for commercial aviation propulsion in the 1960s was dominated by Pratt & Whitney as the dominant market force with almost a 80% market share (on the commercial side of the market) while the market had been growing steadily, which attracted other engine OEMs to it as well.

As discussed earlier, GE's presence in the commercial aviation propulsion market was miniscule, despite of being a powerhouse in the military jets and helicopter engines domain, and was limited to the CJ805, a commercial derivative of its J79 engine, developed in the late 1950s to power the Convair 800 and its sibling, the CJ805-23, developed to power the Convair 900, which later, also featured an aft mounted cruise fan.

However, the Convair story in the commercial aviation history was short lived, despite the fact that the Convair planes were some of the fastest of their era but they failed to make their mark in the highly competitive commercial airlines market. With sales failing to take-off, which coupled with technical challenges being faced by the engines, ultimately led GE to wind up the CJ805 engine program with the last engines delivered to Convair in 1962.

GE Aviation, following the Convair & CJ805 failures, however, was still looking for a comeback trail to the commercial engines market. However, it was not going to be an easy task, even for GE, from any figment of imagination and ultimately it took a span of over half a decade in the 1960s for that opening to appear.

Neumann, GE1 and 'The Building Block' Approach

GE's resurgence, both in the military & commercial aviation market segments, in the second half of 1960s & the company's subsequent market dominance in the 1970s, was scripted & spearheaded by its legendary leader, Gerhard Neumann, who took over the company's reins in 1961. Neumann was better known by his nickname, "Herman the German", which was bequeathed upon him owing to his German ancestry & roots and for the exemplary courage & bravado shown by him while serving actively in China as a propeller specialist with the American Volunteer Group (AVG), which later became the U.S. Army Air Forces during World War II.

Neumann had joined GE in 1948 as a test engineer, wherein, he was recognized for his jet engine innovations, most noticeably, the development of 'variable stator vanes' to prevent compressor stalls on the J79 turbojet engine by fine-tuning air compression at engine inlet. It enabled the Lockheed-built F-104 Starfighter jet to reach a top speed of Mach 2 and a record service ceiling of 100,000 feet, on its own power, which was a first for any production aircraft at the time. Neumann worked with his colleague Neil Burgess & Lockheed's Kelly Johnson, as part of a team, which ultimately won the 1958's Collier Trophy for the breakthrough innovation & the feat.

When Neumann rose to the helm in 1961, GE's market positioning & outlook were weak, bleak & more or less grim, given that the J79 turbojet program, which had powered GE's ascent to prominence in the late 1950s in the military aviation market, did not have long legs to take the company into the technology-led future of military aviation.

Convair's failure in the commercial market had meant the end of the road for GE's first commercial engine the CJ805 while the innovation-laden, J93 military engine program (which was to power the XB-70 bomber program), too, was in limbo following the shelving of the XB-70 even before entering the production stage.

GE's arch-rival, Pratt & Whitney, on the contrary, was dominating the commercial aviation market and had simultaneously also been gaining ground in the military jet propulsion market, especially, after winning the C-141 military transport aircraft program.

GE1, 'the Building Block'

Neumann decided to disrupt the status quo and shake things up inside GE. Backed fully by Jack Parker, GE's Vice Chairman, he radically changed the way things were being done to protect, preserve & enhance GE's market positioning in the jet propulsion market.

GE had always been technologically strong as a company, having assembled the United States' first military jet engine during World War II and had a range of technological innovations readily available at its disposable, given its well-developed military engines portfolio. GE had just developed the propulsion systems for two, state-of-the-art military combat jets of the era, namely, McDonnell's F-4 Phantom II and Lockheed's F-104 Starfighter, both of which had been developed in the late 1950s and were powered by GE's J79 turbojet engines.

However, GE's problems lay in packaging of the cutting edge technologies together, as a collective package, as per a well-defined underlying strategy, in order to meet specific requirements & specifications, especially, on the commercial side of the aviation market, which desperately needed a radical approach like this.

The pathway chosen by Neumann was termed as, the 'building-block' approach, and it was based on a well-established technological roadmap in which a core technology package, containing the most advanced & cutting edge technologies of the times, was readily available which could be harnessed, leveraged or customized, based on its modular architecture, to meet specifications and impending or emerging requirements as per the OEMs.

Neumann & Parker, supported by propulsion stalwarts of the era; including, Peter Kappus, Fred MacFee, Jim Worsham, and Brian T. Rowe, who actively helped towards creation of the technology roadmap; created the GE1 demonstrator engine program in 1962 (originally designated as the X101), which also came to be known as the GE1 'Building Block'.

The GE1 package contained a scaled compressor with variable stator vanes, an innovative annular combustor, advanced technologies for enhanced turbine cooling and multiple material science innovations, which had originally been developed internally by GE for a range of military aircraft programs earlier.

GE1 was a basic gas generator comprising a compressor, combustor and turbine and also was a modular architecture to which a number of components could be added as per the application & requirement. Brian T. Rowe, who helped in the creation of the technology roadmap for GE1, and later also succeeded Neumann to lead GE Aviation, wrote in his autobiography much later about GE1, ""With such an efficient core design as the GE1, we could add a fan or an afterburner or a thrust-vectoring device to satisfy any number of future applications."[13]

The GE1, backed to the hilt by the company's leadership, proved to be the bedrock of GE's R&D efforts going forward and paved the way for the development of multiple new technological innovations and engine core designs, including, the J97 engine, GE1/6 turbofan demonstrator for the TF39 engine, GE4 for the Boeing's proposed 2707 Supersonic passenger airliner in the 1960s (which was later cancelled) and the F101, GE's first afterburning turbofan, which ultimately powered the USAF's B1-B Lancer strategic bomber program. Interestingly, the F101 engine program was the twentieth version of the GE1 core package to reach production stage.

The F101 was later transformed successfully into the F110 engine family, which powered the McDonnell Douglas built F-15E Strike Eagle, General Dynamics' F-16 Fighting Falcon and the Grumman's F-14 Tomcat fighter jets, besides being the basis of the F118 engine, which powered the USAF's B-2 Spirit Bomber.

The F101 was also used to create its civilian variant, the iconic CFM56 engine, which has been one of the most successful commercial engine programs ever, having powered numerous Boeing 737 and Airbus' A320 family aircrafts. However, most significantly, the GE1/6 demonstrator featured the revolutionary core hot section, derived from the GE1, which unlocked the gateway for the genesis and development of a number of military and high-bypass commercial engines going forward.

Neumann's GE1 Building Block, thus, was GE Aviation's ultimate wellspring, which effectively led to the creation of many successful engine programs and enabled GE to effectively take on and compete with arch-rival Pratt & Whitney in the 'Great Engine Wars' over the following decades. Thus, the magnitude of its significance & impact in GE Aviation's history can simply never be stated in just words.

GE Aviations' veterans of the era still maintain that "the GE1 was the greatest GE jet engine to have never powered an aircraft."[44] And the man who spearheaded the creation of the GE1, 'Herman the German', holds a revered place in GE's own corporate history and a very special place in the annals of Aviation history with Neumann duly and deservingly inducted into the National Aviation's Hall of Fame in Dayton, Ohio in 1987. GE Aviation's headquarters in Cincinnati, Ohio has been duly named as, "1 Neumann Way, Evendale", in honor of the visionary man who dared to dream differently and realized it.

His autobiography, "Herman the German: Just Lucky I Guess" would be useful for those looking for a deeper dig on him.

'Building Block' Approach still at Work at GE

It is noteworthy that the building block approach, charted originally by Neumann & Co. in the early 1960s, is still very much at work within GE's Aviation division, even in the 21st century. For instance, the LEAP (Leading Edge Aviation Propulsion) engine program, created by CFM International (GE & Safran's commercial engines JV), to power the next generation of Airbus & Boeing narrow-bodies, as a replacement for the venerable CFM56, was launched in 2008.

The LEAP packs in a number of technological innovations which were originally created by GE Aviation for powering military jets, especially, material science innovations, led by Ceramic Matrix Composites (CMCs), which can operate efficiently at much higher temperatures in the hot sections than the traditional super-alloys.

The LEAP engines' High Pressure (HP) compressor operates at a compression ratio of 22:1, which is almost double than its predecessor, CFM56, leading to a 15% increase in fuel efficiency as compared to its predecessor. LEAP engine's bypass ratio, too, is much higher at almost 11:1 than the CFM56's 6:1.

The LEAP engine also incorporates other revolutionary technologies developed by GE Aviation, including, Oxide-Oxide (OxOx) CMCs that were first researched in the 1980s and were used on the F414 military engine's exhaust seals in 2011 for improved durability.

The same OxOx CMCs found their way into the GE's Passport engine in 2013, which powers Bombardier's Global 7500 & the upcoming Global 8000 business jet, for increased durability & enhanced fuel efficiency with CMCs used in the exhaust section. Passport, thus, became GE's first non-military engine to use the revolutionary technology. The OxOx CMCs have subsequently been used in LEAP engines for commercial airliners as well.

GE is also using its proprietary, 'Super Finish' coating technology, for engine turbine blades, developed for & derived from its military engines, on the Passport and LEAP engines. The 'Super Finish' coating has been used in the High Pressure Compressor (HPC) blades & blisks of the Passport engine, which makes the blades four times smoother than traditional blades, thereby, effectively making the incoming air pass more efficiently over turbine blades resulting in enhanced fuel efficiency.

The Genesis of the TF39 – Heralding of a New Era

In 1963, GE ran its J79 engine core with a much larger front fan, which conceptually would have increased the amount of incoming air, which combined with a smaller engine core and high thermal efficiencies of the combustor operating at high temperatures, a traditional GE expertise, would have efficiently burnt the fuel leading to a high thrust output along with higher fuel efficiencies. It was the basic premise underlying the larger engine, which was became the TF39, and ultimately the CF6.

In 1963, GE pitched the high-bypass engine concept to the USAF for powering the latter's C-5A Galaxy aircraft requirement with GE proposing doubling of the thrust output to 40,000 lbf, which was way more than any contemporary engines of the era. GE's proposal was spearheaded by the company's legendary leader, Gerhard Neumann, who believed that the breakthrough engine design was set to revolutionize air transportation forever.

In 1965, the USAF picked GE's TF-39 turbofan engine over Pratt & Whitney's lower bypass JTF14E, to power the C-5A, a momentous decision which was to bring tectonic shifts in not just military aviation but also was set to transform the market landscape for commercial aviation propulsion market fundamentally.

The TF-39 combined the world's largest front fan, at 97 inches in diameter, creating a high bypass ratio of 8:1, which combined with the unprecedented efficiencies of the compressor, with an overall pressure ratio of 25:1 and high turbine temperatures, translated into a massive technological leap for the industry.

GE declared that the TF-39 would deliver a 25% enhancement in fuel efficiencies, as compared to any of the available large engines of the era, which was ratified in engine test runs later. The advent of the TF39, thus, was a tipping point in the journey of jet propulsion which effectively heralded the era of very large aircrafts, powered by big turbofan engines, capable of globetrotting & covering huge distances efficiently.

GE packed into TF-39, its long list of technological innovations developed over the years, including, air-cooled turbine blades from the J93 engine, aft fan developed for the CJ805-23, the X353-5 lift fan system developed for the Ryan XV-5 Vertifan V/STOL research aircraft (which had a bypass ratio of 12.16:1) and engine core technological breakthroughs from the GE1/6 demonstrator, along with its entire experience, gained through the development of J79 and J85 engines earlier.

The TF-39, thus, was essentially an apotheosis of engine development, reached through the integration of a large series of technological breakthroughs & innovations, created over the years and combined successfully with GE's huge operating experience in developing aircraft engines.

TF-39's Metamorphosis into the CF6

After winning the USAF's C-5 Competition with the TF-39 in 1965, GE announced that it will also be bringing a commercial variant of the TF-39, designated tentatively as the CTF39 at the time. GE Aviation had planned to pursue Douglas, Boeing and Lockheed, to power their future large commercial airliners, with the CTF-39. The CTF39 ultimately became the CF6, which was characterized by a much higher thrust output, lower noise levels and way better fuel efficiency, which was almost 25% higher than its contemporaries. It was designated as the CF6, with the CF denoting GE Aviation's commercial foray while the number 6 denoted the bypass ratio of the new engine.

The development of large engines with high bypass ratios effectively marked the beginning of the end of the turbojets era in commercial aviation and their relegation to the confines of medium range cruise missiles & some other obscure applications ultimately. The short range aircrafts, like regional aircrafts, effectively switched to turboprops operating on limited range routes for better fuel efficiencies. Later, regional jets also appeared powered by turbofans while medium range aircrafts, travelling at high subsonic speeds, have since then, been invariably powered by turbofans.

The overall bypass ratio of the TF39, which powered the USAF's C-5 Galaxy program, was around 8:1 and its ultimate metamorphosis into the CF6 was a major technological breakthrough and a generational leap in terms of potential fuel efficiency gains for the airlines.

Jim Krebs; GE Aviation's engineer, project manager, futurist and a highly revered figure inside GE and in the aviation community; had a key role to play in the transformation of the TF39 into the CF6 with Krebs, along with another GE engineer, Leroy Smith Jr., collectively holding the patent for fan modification on the CF6. Krebs later even told his daughter about his work on the CF6, "I've always been proud of that key component: GE's first commercial front fan"[40]

Krebs had also been the mechanical design manager, working under Gerhard Neumann, who was the head of GE Aviation's jet engine department at the time, in the late 1950s, for the GOL-1590 demonstrator engine developed at Evendale, Ohio which ultimately became the J79 turbojet. He was also

Chapter VII

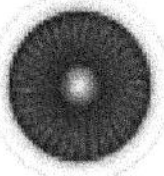

The 'Bees' follow the 'Queen'

The commercial aviation market was booming by 1968 with passenger traffic growing at almost 20% annually and airlines wanted to capitalize on it by acquiring large, wide-body airplanes, on-the-lines of the 747's lucrative operating economics, with seating capacities of around 250 passengers with the capability of traversing large, intercontinental operating ranges, in addition, to the capability of being used efficiently in the domestic market as well.

In 1966, American Airlines floated the requirement for a medium range, wide-body aircraft capable of seating 250 passengers while also being able to haul up to 5,000 pounds of cargo from Chicago to LA. American wanted the aircraft to be relatively smaller than the 747 but capable of flying similar, long range routes while also being capable to operate from airports with shorter runways. United Airlines, too, wanted a 250-seat aircraft for domestic routes and it, too, raised the demand for such a large aircraft.

These airlines quintessentially wanted the attractive operating economics of a twin-jet, capable of carrying 250 passengers on-board along with a sizeable cargo in the belly over long distances in an efficient manner, which had just been pioneered by the 747 but, so far, had been unprecedented in aviation history.

However, none of the engine manufacturers were able to meet the overall thrust requirements with just two engines. Additionally, the FAA's Extended Operations (ETOPS) guidelines were non-existent in the 1960s & 70s, which effectively prevented twin jets from flying transoceanic distances, which would have, thus, essentially, taken intercontinental routes completely out of the operating equation for airlines which would have simply been unfeasible for them.

GE Aviation, having successfully created the CF6, proposed & actively lobbied for the creation of CF6-powered long range, wide-body tri-jets to both Douglas and Lockheed in the late 1960s, after having formally launched the CF6-6 in 1967.

Douglas, however, was going to be the best shot for GE and the CF6 for a commercial market foray, given that, Douglas was eager to expand its aircraft line-up, after the DC-8, but was facing a serious financial crunch.

Lockheed, on the contrary, was largely considered a military market player, having created the C-130 Hercules, C-141 Starlifter and the C-5A Galaxy transport aircrafts for the U.S. military. However, it was devoid of a significant presence in the commercial aircraft market and especially in the jet age.

Further, that same year in 1967, Douglas merged with McDonnell Corporation in 1967, following ongoing financial difficulties at Douglas. This development favored GE Aviation even more as GE had developed the J79 engine for the F-4 Phantom II fighter jet, designed & developed by the McDonnell Corporation a decade ago, in the late 1950s and GE was on good terms with them.

McDonnell Douglas proposed the creation of the DC-10 wide body, single deck tri-jet with a maximum seating capacity of 399 passengers to meet American's requirement while Lockheed, after a long hiatus, almost simultaneously decided to have a go at the commercial airliner market by launching the L-1011 TriStar.

The decision seemed and was a little incongruent with Lockheed's overall strategy given that Lockheed had not produced even a single, jet-powered commercial airliner in the jet age, and its tryst with commercial airplanes had ended long ago since developing the L-188 Electra turboprop way back in 1961.

The DC-10 was to be McDonnell Douglas' fist commercial jetliner following its merger with McDonnell Corporation. In February 1968, American Airlines announced the decision to acquire the DC-10, thereby, becoming the launch customer, along with United Airlines, of the DC-10 with an order for 25 DC-10 aircrafts placed by American while United ordered 30 aircrafts along with an option for another 30 aircrafts.

The Three-Way Battle of Engine OEMs for Aerial Supremacy at the Dawn of the Wide-Body Era

The wide body aircraft market, which was still nascent at the time, suddenly had a triad of capable aircraft contenders and a troika of large, high bypass turbofans to power them with GE's CF6 and Rolls Royce's RB211 turbofan effectively setting up a three-way aerial fray with the first mover, Pratt & Whitney's JT9D.

The RB211 had a thrust output range of 41,000 lbf to 59,450 lbf, essentially covering the same range as the CF6, along with a bypass ratio of 5:1. However, the exorbitant development effort almost pushed Rolls Royce to the brink of bankruptcy, which it somehow averted, through the intervention of the British government.

The high stakes, three-way tactical dogfights for wide body aircraft propulsion (based on turbofans) were, thus, going to be waged between the GE's CF6, Pratt & Whitney's JT9D (later PW4000) and Rolls Royce's RB211 in the trail.

Both DC-10-10 (the initial DC-10 variant) and the L-1011 had almost similar specifications with both tri-jets having a maximum seating capacity of around 400 passengers and a Maximum Take-Off Weight (MTOW) of 430,000 lb. However, the DC-10-10 had an operating range of 3,500 NM while the L-1011 had slightly longer legs with an operating range of 4,000+ NM. The DC-10-10 was to be powered by the GE Aviation's CF6-6 engines producing 40,000 lbf of thrust and almost ready to deploy while Lockheed picked Rolls Royce's still under-development RB211 turbofan.

However, there were stark contrasts in the approaches adopted by McDonnell Douglas for the DC-10-10 and Lockheed for the creation of L-1011 TriStar. McDonnell Douglas, following Douglas' acquisition, took a conservative, cost-oriented approach and wanted the DC-10 to be created on a bare minimum & firm development budget using existing DC-8 technology, with timeline & cost being the core focus areas. McDonnell Douglas, essentially, wanted to be the first one (barring 747) to enter the market with the DC-10, with cost competitiveness as its core forte, in order to gain the first mover advantage.

Lockheed, on the contrary, adopted a technology-oriented focus and took a radical approach to product development, as it was on a comeback trail in the commercial aircraft market and wanted to disrupt the market with the technological innovations it had already developed for military transport aircraft programs or had the internal technological capabilities to create them (leveraging the internal aviation powerhouse, known very well as the 'Skunk Works'). However, Lockheed did not realize that the requirements of commercial market; led, primarily, by procurement & operating costs, are very different from the military market, wherein, costs & economics matter much more than capabilities.

The outcomes of the contrasting approaches undertaken, thus, impinged on the outcomes, which were equally divergent in nature ultimately. The DC-10 had been marred by safety issues with a recurrent cargo door problem which led to multiple, fatal air crashes. The L-1011, on the contrary, was one of the safest aircrafts featuring a full auto-landing capability, which was one of the most sophisticated of the era.

However, McDonnell Douglas with its DC-10-10 beat the L-1011 on entry-into-service timeline, by almost a year, with the DC-10-10's EIS taking place in 1971 while the Rolls Royce's under development RB211 turbofan, chosen as the sole-source engine featuring a radical 3-spool design for reduced drag and a futuristic composite fan, faced technical glitches which ultimately delayed the L-1011's EIS to 1972.

Lockheed's these two tactical errors, of selecting the under development RB211 as the sole-source engine and of packing in a range of exotic technologies (which effectively spiked up its unit price vis-à-vis the DC-10), ultimately shaped the destiny of the L-1011 as a product, which turned out to be actually behind the market cycle, as by the time it entered market, the U.S. economy was facing high inflation levels and the oil crisis was just around the corner, as discussed earlier.

CF6 – 'An Idea whose Time had Come'

The new wide-body aircraft programs & the variants of existing ones, created in the 1970s, were all either powered by the GE's CF6 or at least had it as an engine option, including:-

1. The subsequent variants of the 747, led by the 747-100SR, was created by Boeing in 1972 for the Japanese airlines, which wanted a higher MTOW for increased seating capacity and a shorter operating range. Boeing delivered, while adding the CF6-45 as an engine option, which was continued on the subsequent variants, namely, the 747-200 which ultimately expanded the choice of engine options to 3 for operators, by including, GE Aviation's CF6-50 series and Rolls Royce's RB211-524B engines along with Pratt & Whitney's JT9D-7 series. 747-300, launched in 1980, retained the troika of engine options which was continued on the much upgraded 747-400, one of the most commercially successful 747 variant, launched in the late 1980s. The final 747 variants, 747-8 & its freighter version 747-8F were launched in 2005, leveraging & sharing the 787's wing, cockpit technology & engines. However, it was exclusively powered by the GEnx engines, developed exclusively by GE Aviation, for the 787 program.

2. DC-10's initial variants, the DC-10-10 and the DC-10-30, were powered exclusively by the CF6.

3. Airbus Industrie, the precursor of the current Airbus SE, emerged as a new market force, operating as a collaboration of European aircraft manufacturers, hailing from France, West Germany & the U.K. Airbus decided for a market foray into the large airliner market in 1970 by launching its A300/A310 wide body aircraft family. The A300 was powered by two engine options, namely, Pratt & Whitney's JT9D and GE Aviation's CF6-50/80 which was continued on the A310.

4. Boeing's 767 (launched in 1978) provided operators with an option to choose among GE Aviation's CF6, Rolls Royce's RB211 and Pratt & Whitney's JT9D turbofans. Airbus' A330 wide body program, launched in the 1980s (along with the A340) as an answer to Boeing's 767, was the first Airbus wide body aircraft to provide an option of three engines produced by GE Aviation, Pratt & Whitney and Rolls Royce respectively.

The significant fuel efficiency gains offered by the CF-6, coupled with the emergence of the unprecedented oil crisis in the 1970s, thus, were enough to take the CF-6 to a pre-eminent, pole position in the commercial aviation market within a decade of its foray into commercial aviation in 1968. The GE dynasty, thus, was duly & firmly established in the global wide body aircraft market post GE's CF6 coup.

GE's stupendous success with the CF6 can be effectively gauged from the fact that over the past half a century (1970-2021), GE has already produced almost 8000+ CF6s, which have collectively clocked over 460 million engine flight hours. Further, GE Aviation still has significant, undelivered orders for the CF6 program on its order book while the in-service CF6s are also likely to remain in active service at least through the 2040s.

Contrastingly, it's arch-rival and the market incumbent, Pratt & Whitney's JT9D; having catalyzed the genesis of the era of large, wide body aircrafts, in form of the earlier variants of 747 & followed by the A300/310 and the 767; ended its relatively brief production run in 1990 after having produced almost 3,200 engines. In this regard, we must also contend with and factor-in the fact that Pratt & Whitney had also launched its successor to the JT9D, the PW4000, in the early 1980s, which too, squared off against the CF6 in the 1980s and the 1990s, besides, slugging it out with Rolls Royce's RB211 and the Trent 700.

However, it may not have been the perfect move for Pratt & Whitney, to develop the PW4000, a scratch-up engine development program entailing a huge investment, as part of its underlying plans to capture a larger share of the large commercial engines market pie. This was especially relevant after CF6's advent & meteoric rise, given that, it gave a clear head start to GE in this battle which just seized the initiative from hereupon, simply developed a new engine variant of the CF6 while saving huge sums in R&D investments and gained crucial years in lead over its arch-rival.

Another point to be noted here is that there were no clear & absolute winners in these three way battles waged between Pratt & Whitney, GE Aviation and Rolls Royce for supremacy of the commercial aviation's large engines market. The initial variants of all these engines, namely, the JT9D, CF6 and the RB211, clearly had teething troubles and technical issues during early phases of their entry into service, which were subsequently addressed and rectified as they came up, with the subsequent engine versions duly incorporating those redesigns, modifications as well as changes, resulting in three equally capable and worthy engine rivals, which fought among them tooth and nail for market shares at least throughout the 1970s decade...

Chapter VIII

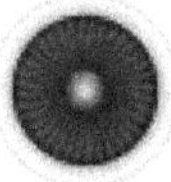

A 'Heavenly' Match

The CF6's success underscored GE's successful foray into the global commercial aircraft engines market. However, GE wanted to further capitalize on it by developing and bringing a medium thrust engine to the market, in the 20,000 lbf to 30,000 lbf thrust class, which would have essentially powered the narrow body aircrafts.

The move, initiated in the early 1970s, was targeted at the replacement or re-engining of the in-service fleets of Boeing's 707 & 727 and the Douglas' DC-8 & DC-9 aircrafts, all of which had entered the market in the late 1950s or early 1960s and were powered either by the Pratt & Whitney's JT3D or the JT8D (727 & DC-9).

Additionally, there was also the significant market potential of re-engining the military variants derived from commercial aircrafts, especially, the USAF's KC-135 tankers, E-3 Sentries and the E-8 JSTARS, all of which were based on Boeing's 707 platform. They were powered either by the Pratt & Whitney's J57 turbojet (KC-135A) or the TF33 (E-3 Sentry and the E-8 JSTARS), which is also found on the B-52H Stratofortress. However, these first generation turbofans (TF33/JT3D) and the J-57 turbojet were noisy and inefficient and would have needed re-engining with newer engines as part of their mid-life upgrades.

GE Aviation's legend, Jim Krebs, recounted the following regarding GE's move towards medium thrust engine, which eventually turned out to be the CFM56, while being interviewed for the book "CFM: The Power of Flight", authored by Guy Norris and Felix Torres, "I decided that we would undertake the design of an all-new, advanced, high-bypass turbofan engine in the 20,000-pound thrust class" to power "the next round of medium transports."[40] It is important to note that Krebs was at the time the head of GE Aviation's internal think tank, APPO, which undertook such strategic decisions.

The European aerospace industry, too, had been well developed by the late 1960s and had effectively demonstrated its engineering prowess by having developed the world's first supersonic passenger airliner, Concorde, with the French Snecma (now Safran Aircraft Engines) and the British Bristol Siddeley (which was ultimately acquired by Rolls Royce in 1966) having jointly developed the Olympus 593 high performance turbojet engine for it successfully.

Snecma, which had so far primarily been focused on military engines, had been looking actively for a foray into the commercial side, following its acquisition of Hispano-Suiza, a French aerospace company in 1968, and had even pursued a commercial engine study in 1969, designated as M56, under a French government directive for the further development of commercial aviation capabilities in the nation. Snecma, however, had been looking for a suitable industry partner and had Pratt & Whitney, Rolls Royce and GE Aviation on its radar, for a market foray via the JV route.

For both GE & Snecma, but especially for GE, the JV would have reduced the capital outlay required for new engine's development, reduced the financial & technological risks involved and would have enabled it to cater to rapid internationalization of commercial aviation, underway at the time.

For Snecma, the JV would have enabled it to leverage GE Aviation's technological expertise in the commercial aviation market, following the market success of the CF6, which had debuted on the DC-10. Additionally, GE Aviation and Snecma had already been working together on powering the A300, the world's first wide body twin-jet, which had its EIS in October 1972, with the addition of CF6-50 as an engine option (in addition to the JT9D), which had been done to appeal to U.S. based airlines. Snecma had already been producing parts for the CF6-50s, produced by GE, for the Airbus' A300 & the DC-10s sold in Europe.

GE's participation in the USAF's Advanced Medium STOL Transport (AMST) program in 1972, wherein, it was competing head-on with Pratt & Whitney and Rolls Royce, included the development of a medium thrust class engine based on cutting-edge technologies.

Initially, GE Aviation wanted to base the new medium thrust commercial engine, to be developed jointly with Snecma, on the commercial technology derived from the CF6. However, GE simultaneously also feared that a potential loss on the USAF program, going forward, would leave it with a medium class commercial engine, devoid of the technological advances it had already developed over its F101 engine (based on the GE 1 Building block), created for Rockwell's B-1 Lancer supersonic bomber program, as per USAF's requirement.

GE ultimately decided to use the F101's engine core as the basis for deriving the new medium thrust commercial engine, along with Snecma, while seeking U.S. government clearance for the export of F101 engine core, which was deemed as sensitive technology and would have been the biggest roadblock in GE's grand plan.

Interestingly, Jim Krebs was present here, too, behind the scenes as he himself had shaped the development of the F101 engine program for the B-1 supersonic bomber as GE Aviation's Vice President of the military engine programs, a stint, wherein, he also oversaw the development of engines for the F-117 Night Hawk, USA' first stealth fighter built by Lockheed, besides, the B-2 Spirit bomber, UH-60 Black Hawk & AH-64 Apache helicopters, A-10 Warthog, S-3A Viking and the F-18 Hornet fighter jet.

GE's plans to use the F101 core, however, were thwarted by the denial of export license by the U.S. regulatory authorities in 1972, on the grounds of it being a sensitive technology, already in use in a strategic program and critical to national defense & security.

Additionally, the F-101 engine had been developed with the R&D funding provided by the Department of Defense (DOD) for use on the USAF's B-1 program. Thus, without the U.S. Government's clearance, the plans for the development of a new, medium-duty commercial engine, derived from it, would have been in limbo.

The U.S. government, however, ultimately relented to the relentless lobbying & campaigning by GE Aviation with their argument that denying it the export license would ultimately threaten America's technological & aerospace dominance going forward as the French would develop the engine on their own and would go on to create a market dominance in the medium thrust engines market in commercial aviation.

In April 1970, a delegation of Snecma's top executives visited GE Aviation leaders in Boston, MA with the JV idea being at the back of their mind which was duly shared and discussed over the course of drinks and meals.

However, it took another 4 years of tough negotiations, detailed outlining of work share agreements and governmental clearances to make things tick, with the creation of CFM International, the 50:50 owned JV entity, duly formed in 1974.

The naming of the jointly owned entity, as CFM International, is also interesting as it combines the initials CF, derived from GE's CF6 engine program with the initial letter of Snecma's M56 study, conducted earlier for commercial engine foray. The first engine offspring of the JV, too, thus, was duly named as CFM56 (which will be covered a little later).

However, contrary to popular beliefs, the JV creation, too, was a two-way contest with Pratt & Whitney very much being a prominent character in the saga. Snecma had, in fact, been in active talks with both GE Aviation and Pratt & Whitney for the potential JV, at the time, with both the companies having submitted their proposals duly for the same.

As per Jack Connors, Pratt & Whitney's program manager for legacy engine programs, who has mentioned it in his book[6], "Pratt & Whitney had a 10.9% ownership stake in Snecma and even had a seat on the French company's board at the time. Snecma and Pratt & Whitney had signed an agreement in 1960 for the manufacture & sale of Pratt & Whitney's gas turbine engines and complete line-up of piston engines by Snecma, which gave Pratt & Whitney a 10.9% equity stake in the French company along with a board seat. However, the factor that ultimately turned the tide in GE's favor for the JV was the fact that GE was offering an advanced engine core from a military program developed under DOD funding, had cutting edge technology in it with better marketing prospects and was readily available, as against Pratt & Whitney, whose proposal was based on a contemporary, commercial engine technology. The fortune, somehow, just favored GE Aviation at the time."[6]

The CFM56 was developed as a high-bypass turbofan engine, with its bypass ratio ranging from 5:1 to 6:1 across variants and thrust output ranging from 18,500 lbf to 34,000 lbf, which is the typical range required to power twin-jet narrow bodies even today.

The first CFM56 engine, dubbed as the CFM56-2, had its maiden run in mid-1974 at a GE facility with the second engine exported to France in late 1974. The CFM56, however, had its maiden flight three years later in 1977, when one of the four JT8D engines on the McDonnell Douglas' YC-15 test aircraft, developed as a tactical transport aircraft with STOL capability for a USAF program, was replaced with a CFM56 engine and it roared on its way to the sky.

The CFM56, however, despite being backed by GE Aviation and the French Government, as Snecma was owned by the French Government (at the time) as a state owned enterprise, had a very difficult market foray commercially as the program did not find any initial takers in its early years, following the market launch in 1974. As discussed earlier, the CFM56 program had been targeting the potential market opportunity of re-engining the McDonnell Douglas' DC-8 and Boeing's 707, along with its military variants, especially, the USAF's KC-135 Stratotanker, which was the prime target on the company's radar, given the huge, in-service fleet size of KC-135s, numbered at around 600 aircrafts at the time.

The CFM56 engine, however, was technically way advanced & ahead of its time technologically, absolutely as well as relatively. Pratt & Whitney's JT8D engine, which was the predominant & incumbent engine for narrow bodies in the 1960s & 1970s, was a low bypass turbofan engine with a bypass ratio of mere 0.96:1, as compared to CFM56's 5:1, translating into relatively way higher fuel efficiency and low noise levels for the CFM56. The former, especially, would have proved to be really significant for the 1970s decade, given the completely unexpected advent of the Global Oil Crisis, which led to an unprecedented surge in oil prices globally.

However, the aspect, which did not favor the CFM56 engine was that it had not been developed and launched to power a specific, under development commercial or military aircraft program but rather for re-engining the older, in-service narrow bodies. The decisions for such undertakings are usually dictated by strategic stakeholders & market forces and usually entail long drawn processes.

Secondly, the late 1960s and the 1970s was the era of large wide-bodies which were used to carry hordes of passengers over long distance efficiently, which had led to the rise of 747 followed by the DC-10, Lockheed-1011 and the Airbus' A300/310 respectively. The market size & growth potential for narrow bodies at the time, thus, was relatively very limited as compared to the wide bodies, especially in an era, wherein, the airlines industry was highly regulated.

The leading narrow body aircraft programs of the 1960s era, namely, the DC-8 & the DC-9 along with Boeing's sole tri-jet, 727, were all powered by the Pratt & Whitney's JT3D (DC-8) & JT8D engines. Boeing had launched its 737 twin-jet narrow body program in 1965, powered by the JT8D engines, which ultimately entered service in 1967.

However, Boeing really had struggled to sell the 737, right from its EIS in 1967 till almost 1973, a phase, wherein, the DC-8s & DC-9s were outselling the 737 by almost 3:1. Further, by then, Boeing was almost on the verge of winding up the 737 program and even was considering selling it to the Japanese aviation industry, owing to financial difficulties being encountered over the huge development costs & significant capital expenditure incurred on the 747 program, which had almost pushed Boeing onto the verge of bankruptcy.

The decision to develop & launch a medium-thrust engine in the turbulent decade of 1970s, without a direct aircraft application, and primarily on the market potential of re-engining older narrow bodies, while incurring significant capital investments, was either highly visionary or extremely reckless on the part of CFM International and its leaders who had backed the program fully and given it the green light without a specific & actual, immediate commercial or military application. The destiny of the CFM56 program, thus, was truly in the hands of market forces and the rapidly changing Aviation zeitgeist of the time.

Theoretically & technically, the decision to launch the CFM56 was sound, given the enormous potential it had to disrupt the market as the world's first truly high bypass medium thrust turbofan, entailing a huge promise of substantially higher fuel efficiencies as compared to the low bypass JT8D, which would have been no match for the relatively way superior, CFM56.

Secondly, the commercial aviation industry's evolution has traditionally been led & shaped by the periodic advancements in engine technology, which has consistently predated & catalyzed the launch of new commercial aircraft programs, throughout aviation history.

The commercial aviation landscape in the 1970s, however, despite grappling with multiple challenges & headwinds, was on the verge of a major revolution owing to two key market developments in the late 1970s, which originated from the regulatory side, and were to provide significant tailwinds to the CFM56 program going forward and take it on to the path of market ascendancy to ultimate supremacy eventually.

They were, passing of the regulatory act for controlling noise regulations for aircrafts & airports and the deregulation of aviation industry in the U.S in the 1978, respectively. The surge in oil prices during the 1970s oil crisis became another key factor which helped CFM56's case owing to its high bypass ratio and much better fuel efficiency as compared to the previous generation, low bypass turbofans.

Let's visit them to understand as to how they favored & actually propelled the CFM56 program on its way to ultimate market supremacy in the medium thrust engines market...

Chapter IX

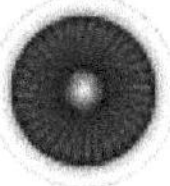

The 'Noisy' Affair

Noise Regulations at the Dawn of the Jet Age

Prior to the dawn of the jet age commercially in the U.S. market in the late 1950s, with the Boeing 707 (which was preceded by the development of Caravelle jets in France & the Comet 4 in the U.K.), air travel was essentially propeller-driven, with Douglas' DC-7, Lockheed's Super-G Constellation and Boeing's 377 Stratocruiser ruling the roost, and coast-to-coast air travel across the United States taking almost 8 hours.

However, even in the propeller era, noise was an acknowledged problem, especially for the residents, who had their houses located close to and around key airports. An article published in the 2007's edition of the Sound & Vibration magazine has a great back story on the same titled, "The Noisy Dawn of the Jet Age"[14] It mentions that, even before the jet age, the regulatory authorities had already directed the aircraft manufacturers to suppress noise levels of their aircrafts even way back in 1951 and had even stipulated a measure to ban all aircrafts not meeting the noise level requirements.

The article mentions that in 1956, the Port of New York Authority (PNYA) executives, along with the director of civil aviation and other stakeholders, presided over a meeting, convened for taking a decision whether to allow operations of jet aircrafts from the New York International Airport at Idlewild (now JFK). The recorded minutes of that meeting exactly mention, "Pan American Airways has asked for permission to begin jet aircraft operations from Idlewild airport in November 1958. They will be flying a new jet passenger airplane, called the Boeing 707. We must know how noisy it is. We already have a lawsuit in progress at our Newark airport brought on by residents who are complaining about the noise from today's propeller airplanes. The noise surrounding Idlewild must not be worse than that created by present large propeller-driven airplanes."[14]

The director of civil aviation, John Wiley, remarked, "Several years ago, we told the airlines that a jet plane must make no more noise than a large propeller airplane on takeoffs and landings. Boeing claims that they have met this requirement and their evidence is that the conventional sound level meter shows the same number of decibels of noise from the jet plane during flyover as from a Super-Constellation propeller airplane. But we are worried, because we are getting reports that the 707 is much noisier. In fact, we have already received threats that if the noise around Idlewild increases, mothers with baby strollers will go on to the runways."[14] An investigation was called for and assigned to the Bolt Beranek and New-man, Inc., referred to as BBN.

The findings of the study report were shocking, which concluded, that the jet aircraft operations were way more noisier than the propeller planes given that the noise emitted (measured in perceived noise in decibels or PNdB) by propeller planes is in the low-frequency range of 50 to 200 Hz. while the noise created by jet aircrafts was found to be in the high-frequency range of 500 Hz to 2,000 Hz. (as reported in the article).

The problem was further compounded by the well-known fact that human hearing is way more sensitive to high-frequency sounds, as compared to low-frequency noise. BBN & PNYA found the difference between the noise levels of propeller aircrafts and the 707 to be of 15 dB, which was considered as substantial & unacceptable.

Boeing was informed of the same and the company started working towards mechanisms to reduce noise levels by using mufflers & other mechanical noise suppression mechanisms. However, incorporating heavier mufflers would have added weight, which would have impacted the 707's performance characteristics, including, operating range, payload capacity and/or fuel efficiency.

In the meanwhile, Air France sought PYNA's permission in 1957 to use Idlewild airport for its Caravelle jets, as part of its proposed Paris-Idlewild flight route. PYNA informed them of the noise level restrictions for jets at play which had to be equivalent to the propeller powered aircrafts, in order, to be acceptable.

Air France pilots, however, took a very different approach to take-offs using their Caravelle jets. They would take-off and after getting airborne, would climb at the rate of 1:5 with engine rpm maintained at 8,000 levels, till they reached an altitude of 1,200 ft. Subsequently, they would cut-off power to 7,100 rpm and would climb at a ratio of 1:17 to an altitude of about 1,300 ft.

With this approach to take-off, the perceived noise level in decibel (PNdB) of the Caravelle jets was found to be the same as propeller powered aircrafts, as measured & reported by BBN & PYNA engineers. Following this, the Caravelle jets were cleared & permitted to use the Idlewild airport routinely for flight operations using this approach in May 1957, which was later also extended to the British Comet jets, in August 1958 using the same approach.

Boeing was asked by the PYNA to follow the same take-off approach with its 707s, as was being used by Air France's Caravelles and the British Comet 4 jets. However, even with its best mufflers and using the same take-off approach, 707's noise levels were still way above the acceptable limit.

The PYNA & BBN executives then studied & measured the perceived noise levels (PNdB) coming off a Comet 4 aircraft operating from Idlewild to ascertain an appropriate PNdB level for the surrounding neighborhoods. It was collectively ascertained & unanimously agreed to be 112 PNdB, which was officially accepted as the upper limit, and was also duly published in the official PYNA report that came out in early October 1958, without major repercussions or lawsuits from airlines.

A news piece appearing in 'The Wall Street Journal' the very next day mentioned, "The New York Port Authority gave permission on October 3 for jet flights at Idlewild. The restrictions are: a) in good weather use runways over water. b) in bad weather make turns to the right as soon as possible. c) If the flight must go over communities, do so at 1200 ft, with engines throttled back, accompanied by turns. d) All take-offs between 10 p.m. and 7 a.m. must be over water. An exhaustive 170 page booklet was published by Bolt, Be-ranek and Newman (BBN)."[14]

The implementation of a clear upper limit on the acceptable noise levels at the very dawn of the jet age meant active & constant pursuit of ongoing efforts by the industry, subsequently, led by the engine OEMs, to reduce or suppress noise levels. The most critical part of addressing the Gordian knot, thus, became the development of high bypass ratio turbofans which effectively reduced noise levels by controlling the volume of air going into the engine core as compared to the part bypassing it owing to the frontal fan. The 747's noise level, developed in the late 1960s, thus, was 20 EPNdB[14] (Effective Perceived Noise in Decibels) lower as compared to the late 1950s-era 707, while the 777, developed in the early 1990s, was even 10 EPNdB[14] more quieter than the 747.

Further Tightening of Aircraft Noise Levels in the Early 1970s – ICAO as the Apex Body

Today's International Civil Aviation Organization or the ICAO, the global regulatory body for civil aviation, had its genesis in the Chicago Convention signed on December 07, 1944 by its 52 member states leading to the creation of the Provisional International Civil Aviation Organization, or the PICAO, with 26 member states yet to ratify the convention.

The ICAO duly came into existence from the PICAO on April 04, 1947 with "mutual agreement among governments of member states on certain principles & arrangements for the development of international civil aviation in a safe and orderly manner"[15], as its duly stated raison d'etre.

The ICAO Council was instructed by the 16th ICAO Assembly, held in 1968, to focus on aircraft noise by developing international specifications & associated guidance material. The ICAO Council was ordered to develop methods to describe and measure aircraft noise, including, suitable limitations on aircraft- generated noise and its impact on communities residing in the vicinity of airports.

In 1969, ICAO Council's "Special Meeting on Aircraft Noise in the Vicinity of Aerodromes" was convened in Montreal, from November 25, 1969 to December 17, 1969, for defining the technical specifications and development of noise measurement criteria. In August 1971, the ICAO Council duly adopted the first edition of Annex 16 – Aircraft Noise, thereby, which became the first global environmental standard applicable to new airplane designs.

Another important development was the acknowledgement of noise generated by aircrafts, as a function of their Maximum Take-off Mass (MTOM), as the appropriate criteria leading to differentiation of noise standards for small and large airplanes.

FAA & the U.S. Congress Come into Play

Following the passing of ICAO Council's Annex 16, the Federal Aviation Administration (FAA) developed and implemented its regulation on aircraft noise emissions, under its Title 14 of the Code of Federal Regulations (14 CFR) Part 36, "Noise Standards: Aircraft Type and Airworthiness Certification" in 1969, which had to be complied with by airplanes in order to receive their new or revised 'Type' certification, also referred to as 'Airworthiness' certificate to be able to operate successfully in the U.S.

However, the initial set of emission rules, outlined in 1969, were only applicable to large aircrafts operating in the transport category powered by turbojet engines and were subsequently revised & expanded to include other categories in the 1970s. The noise limits were defined in "Effective Perceived Noise Level" or EPNL or EPNdB.

The U.S. Congress, following the FAA's passing of noise regulations, passed the 'Aircraft and Airport Noise Reduction Act' in July 1978, which mandated "the Secretary of Transportation to establish a single system of measuring noise and the impact of noise on individuals to be used to measure noise at airports and their surrounding areas"[16].

The act also "Directed the Federal Aviation Administration to require all aircraft operated by international operators in the United States to meet the noise level standards contained in part 36 of title 14, Code of Federal Regulations, or annex 16 of the International Civil Aviation Organization (ICAO)."[16]

The regulatory tightening & emergence of stringent regulations for noise emissions in the 1970s, however, arrived almost as a tectonic shift which shook things up fundamentally and impacted industry players in an asymmetric manner, as usual, by presenting significant opportunities & tailwinds to some industry players & market forces while posing serious, existential threats to others as headwinds...

Chapter X

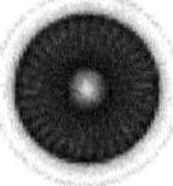

The 'Breakthrough'

The dawn of the jet age had brought noisy and inefficient turbojets & low-bypass turbofans with it, derived from their military counterparts, to commercial airports and their surroundings. Anyone who has ever heard a Rolls Royce Conway or the Pratt & Whitney's J57 (which was the basis of the JT3D low-bypass turbofan for commercial operations which powered the 707s & DC-8s commercial airliners & the KC-135E Stratotanker & B-52H Stratofortress military aircrafts) powered jet take-offs or landings in the late 1950s or 1960s would remember as to how loud those engines were. In fact, the J57 powered KC-135A was the noisiest aircraft in the entire USAF fleet with wet take-offs generating a huge noise output of 165 db[17].

A typical commercial airplane powered by a turbofan engine usually & typically generates a noise output, ranging from 80 db to 110 db across its flight stages, including, take-off, straight/level flight and landing approach. Interestingly, that's within the 112 PNdB range, as determined and fixed by the PYNA, way back in 1958. A typical Boeing 707-100B quad-jet in the late 1950s era, which would come closest to a modern narrow body jet, with a MTOW of 200,000 lb. powered by Pratt & Whitney's early JT3D-1 engines produced a noise output of 95.5 dB during take-off phase (TO), 99.5 dB during straight/level flight phase (SL) and 101 dB during its landing approach phase (AP), based on FAA data[18].

The Case for CFM56 – Promise of Lower Noise and Higher Fuel Efficiencies

On a head-to-head comparison basis, based on specifications, the CFM56 engine was almost 20% more fuel efficient than the JT8D and 25% more fuel efficient than the JT3D, as per Boeing. The CFM56 also was relatively much quieter than the JT8D, in addition to being way more fuel efficient, given its high bypass ratio of 5:1 as compared to JT8D's 0.93:1.

The FAA's database[18] on aircraft & engine noises (dating to the year 2012), further mentions that a CFM56 powered 737-300 had a 10 dB lower noise output at take-off, than a 737-200 powered by the JT8D, with both aircrafts having the same MTOW. The challenger CFM56, thus, truly was a market disruptor in the medium thrust engines market, based on its technological advancement, generationally & in overall capabilities, when compared to the JT8D in a direct, apples-to-apples comparison.

On a comparative basis, Boeing's first generation 737-200 ADV twin-jet, with a MTOW of 124,500 lb. powered by the P&W's JT8D-15 engines generated a noise output of 91.8 dB during TO, 96.7 dB during SL and 96.3 dB during AP phases respectively as per the FAA as of 2012[18]. However, a 737-300, with an exactly same MTOW, powered by the CFM56-3 engines (with HWFAP) had almost a 10 dB lower (except approach phase) noise output level of 82.4 dB (-10 dB) for TO, 89.7 for SL (-7 dB) and 98.5 dB (+2.2 dB) for its AP phases as per FAA's 2012 data[18]

The original JT8D, however, incorporated an exhaust mixer developed especially by Pratt & Whitney engineers, which effectively mixed the high velocity, noisier air exhaust from the turbine discharge with the low velocity, low noise air exhaust of the bypass duct resulting in a slight overall noise reduction of almost 6 dB for the JT8D engine.

The device was made available as a hush kit (which was costing almost $2.8 million[25] in the 1990s) which proved to be successful with almost 77%[6] of the JT8D operators ended up using the hush kits for complying with prevailing noise regulations.

The CFM56, thus, was the heavyweight of the medium thrust engines market segment while the JT8D could at best be termed as the middleweight. However, the CFM56, too, was not infallible and had its weak spot and it was its unit cost. The CFM56 engine's unit cost was almost 25% more than that of the JT8D, given the incorporation of advanced materials and the incorporation of additional engine stages for the much higher bypass ratio it generated.

In the commercial aviation market, competitiveness, based on overall economics, is the paramount parameter for success, which is sometimes, given even more importance than safety, as was shown by the market's preference for the McDonnell Douglas' DC-10, which was available at a much lower procurement cost as compared to the way-more safer but also more expensive, L-1011.

CFM56's Initial Tryst with the Commercial Aviation Market

Following the CFM56-2's market debut in 1974, which did not get a much enthusiastic response from the market as the DC-9s and Boeing's 737-100 & -200, powered by the JT8D engines, had just entered the market in the 1960s and not ripe for re-engining.

Secondly, the relatively higher unit cost of the CFM56, which clearly was in incongruence with the high profit orientation of the highly bottom-line focused commercial airlines, was a huge disincentive for them, especially, in the absence of any regulatory requirements requiring their usage. The CFM56, thus, expectedly, did not find any takers during its initial years.

In 1977, Boeing showed an interest in the CFM56 engine for its 707 aircraft platform, as it was aware of the tighter noise regulations which were being mulled by the Congress, which were just round the corner and almost imminent. The new, more stringent noise regulations were enacted formally as an act, within a year, in 1978.

Boeing, being a first-hand victim and having gone through the ordeal as well as the compliance burden of noise standards in 1958 itself (as discussed in the previous chapter), was already anticipating the move and had been proactively exploring possible solutions to meet stricter noise requirements. The CFM56, thus, was expectedly, at the top of Boeing's list. Boeing formally announced the mounting of CFM56 engines on a 707-320 aircraft for the purpose of conducting flight tests.

CFM56 and Military Aviation

As discussed earlier, the military aviation market, on the contrary to commercial, is driven by performance & capabilities mix being offered by the technology, as the primary factor & parameter for decision-making, rather than mere procurement or operating economics and, thus, would have been a right fit for a market disruptive technology, like the CFM56.

The U.S. Air Force (USAF) had been operating its KC-135A tankers (based on the Boeing's Dash 80 or 367-80 prototype which also produced the 707) powered by the Pratt & Whitney's J57 engines. However, these engines were extremely noisy & highly inefficient, which even the USAF itself acknowledged while issuing an RFP for their re-engining later in 1977.

Conceptually, the CFM56 would have been a perfect fit for the USAF's KC-135s, as technologically, it was the best possible contender for re-engining, as compared to the TF33 & the JT8D engines, being offered by rival Pratt & Whitney.

For CFM56, winning a re-engining contract from the USAF was critical, as it would have provided the program with a much needed & highly required launch order as well as boost, given the overall size & scope of the program. The USAF had an active, in-service fleet of almost 600 KC-135As, which would have needed 4 engines each, in addition, to the substantial & recurring, incoming revenue streams, in form of MRO revenues, which the contract would have brought over the subsequent years.

Boeing, in the meanwhile, also developed the 707-700 in 1979, purely as an experimental variant of 707 featuring CFM56-2 engines mated to the original 707 airframe, in order, to explore & test the potential re-engining scenario for the 707. The tests were successful but Boeing did not proceed any further towards offering the 707-700 commercially to its airlines customers, as the company felt, that doing so could potentially cannibalize the market prospects for its upcoming 757 narrow body jet, which was launched in 1978. However, Boeing's testing of the CFM56 engines on the 707 airframe did pave the way for and helped build the case for re-engining of the USAF's KC-135As with CFM56 engines.

The case for re-engining of KC-135s with France-made CFM56 engines was further supported by the French government's decision to re-engine its 11 in-service KC-135s with the CFM56 engines in 1978 which almost came as a shot in the arm for the program.

Further, in 1978 only, NATO, too, placed an order for 18 E-3D AWACS aircrafts with Boeing worth $1.8 billion. The E-3D, too, was derived from the Boeing's 707 airframe and the NATO's planes were to be powered by the CFM56-2 engines[38], as requested by NATO, which provided further tailwinds to the CFM56 engine program. These aircrafts ultimately entered service in the early 1980s with 7 operated by the Royal Air Force in the U.K. while 4 went to France and some to Germany.

The passing of the Aircraft and Airport Noise Reduction Act by the U.S. Congress in July 1978 effectively paved the way and provided the business case for re-engining of older aircrafts, being operated by the airlines, especially the older & noisy DC-8s, in order, to meet the upcoming, stringent noise requirements,.

It surely came as a boon for the CFM56 program, which was just weeks away and almost on the verge of being put on the chopping block, as it had not been able to secure even a single order from the commercial aircraft market, so far, since the program's launch in 1974.

However, in April 1979, almost a couple of months after the French and NATO contracts for CFM56 powered aircrafts, United Airlines announced its decision to re-engine 30 of its DC-8-61 aircrafts with the CFM56 engines, marking a decisive and pivotal victory in the commercial market for the CFM56 program in its almost half a decade long struggle for a potential market entry.

The United's decision was followed by the decision by Delta Airlines to re-engine its DC-8-61s, dating back to the late 1950s & 1960s, with the CFM56 engine, which effectively led to the creation of the DC-8-71 series. Delta's decision to re-engine its DC-8s was based on its internal assessment that the DC-8 was the only aircraft type readily available in the market which was capable of undertaking some specific domestic routes, with a given payload factor, and without any other competing aircraft program being available given that the 767 was still being conceived by Boeing while Lockheed had effectively abandoned its TriStar 400 program and completely exited the commercial market.

The cargo giant, Flying Tiger Line, too, soon followed suit and announced the decision to re-engine its DC8-63F freighters, dating back to the late 1960s, with the CFM56 engines. The re-engining of the Boeing's 707, however, remained limited to its military variants only, as Boeing essentially wanted to safeguard its upcoming 757s & 767s from cannibalization threats. Further, Boeing had clearly anticipated the upcoming era of twin jets, in which, the older, narrow body quad jets, even post re-engining, would have clearly been a misfit from the perspective of operating economics.

In the early 1980, the USAF announced its decision of going with the CFM56 engines for re-engining KC-135As, with CFM International formally announced as the winner of the high-stakes contest, which came as a massive victory for the CFM56 program. The CFM56, which was desperately looking for a substantial foothold in the market, in order to secure its future just a year ago, thus, was here to stay and rise as a true disruptor and a key market force.

CFM56 Fulfills its Destiny

The re-engining of the DC-8s and the KC-135s with the CFM56, with re-engined KC-135s designated as the KC-135R, brought in significant capability enhancements to the DC-8s and the USAF's KC-135s. Delta's DC-8-71s reported a 23%[21] increase in fuel efficiency as compared to the erstwhile Pratt & Whitney JT3Ds, along with lower noise levels and an increase in power. Further, the operating range of these DC-8s also increased by a huge margin of 3,300[21] NM to 6,500[21] NM which effectively brought in significant gains DC-8's primary operators, namely, Delta & United.

Delta, in fact, became the world's first airline operator to offer CFM56-2 based commercial passenger service in April 1982 using its DC-8-71s which connected Atlanta and Savannah. Overall, a total of 110 older DC-8-60s were re-engined to DC-8-71, -72 & -73 with the CFM56-2 engines between 1979 and 1988 with the conversions carried out by Cammacorp. Interestingly, 2 of these converted DC-8-73s are still in active commercial service with Skybus Jet Cargo, a Peru-based cargo airline, as of January 2023.

USAF ultimately re-engined 500 of its KC-135s with the CFM56 engines while the remaining 100 odd aircrafts, operated by the Air National Guard and Air Force Reserve, were re-engined with the Pratt & Whitney's used TF33 engines in 1978, which became available following the retirement of Boeing's 707 commercial aircrafts in late 1970s & 1980s, and were designated as KC-135E.

The re-engined KC-135Rs had a 27% better fuel efficiency[19] along with 30% increase in thrust[19] and they could carry up to 50% more[19] fuel on their refueling missions. They also reported a reduction in operating costs to the tune of almost 25%[19] as compared to the USAF's original KC-135s powered by TF33s.

The incorporation of CFM56 engines also effectively reduced the noise level of KC-135Rs at take off to 99 decibels[19] from 126 decibels earlier. Further, the KC-135R's operating range is almost 60% more than KC-135E while carrying similar fuel loads and also offering lower overall operating costs.

The USAF remains CFM International's biggest customer with almost 2,000[20] CFM56 engines in service, thereby, making it one of the most successful re-engining programs in aviation history, while also having provided a good enough runway to the CFM56 program to take-off from, along with enough propulsion, to take it on an unanticipated & adventurous journey from an obscure, insignificant existence to absolute market dominance over the course of the next 2+ decades...

CFM56 Engine Variants Developed through the 1980s

CFM56-2 for 707's Military Variants and the DC-8 Super 70

The CFM56-2 engine, with a thrust output range of 22,000 to 24,000 lbf, went on to become one of the most popular engines in the air, owing to its sturdiness, high efficiency & reliability. It was also the first high bypass turbofan engine which was custom-built for the 10-ton engine class, almost exclusively for the narrow bodies and became a sort of wellspring for the creation of subsequent engine variants of the CFM56 family.

Apart from the USAF's KC-135R, the CFM56-2 engine also powered two other military variants derived from the 707, namely, E-3 Sentry AWACS and the E-6B. Additionally, the DC-8 Super 70, the re-engined variant of the DC-8 created in the late 1970s & 1980s, also sported the CFM56-2 engine.

CFM56-3 for Boeing's 737 Classic Aircraft Family

The CFM56-3 was created specifically for the Boeing's 737 Classic aircraft family in the early 1980s, comprising the 737-300,-400 and -500 aircraft programs. It was created when Boeing decided to re-engine the 737 Original and expand the 737 family's aircraft line-up while incorporating additional technological upgrades in the late 1970s. The 737 Classic family entered service powered by the CFM56-3 engine, with a thrust output range of 18.500 to 23,500 lbf, in 1984.

CFM56-5A for Airbus' A320 Aircraft Family

Another variant of the CFM56 engine, the CFM56-5A, was developed for the Airbus' A320 aircraft family, which was launched with the A320ceo program in 1984 and entered service in 1988, powered by the CFM56-5-A1 engine. The thrust output of the CFM56-5A ranged from 22,000 lbf to 26,500 lbf.

CFM56-5C for the Airbus' A340 Wide Body Aircraft Program

The largest member of the CFM56 engine family, the CFM56-5C, came into existence to power the Airbus' A340 wide body quadjet, which was launched in 1987. The CFM56-5C variant had a thrust output range of 31,200 lbf to 34,000 lbf and powered the A340-200 and A340-300 aircraft variants, which entered service in 1993.

A company press release by CFM International, titled, "CFM56 Engines: The Standard to which Others are Judged", issued in September 1996, perfectly captures the achievements of the CFM56 engine program in a nutshell and how it had almost become an industry benchmark in itself with its unmatched reliability and on-wing records.

The press release proudly mentions, with duly earned bragging rights, "Every seven seconds, a CFM56-powered aircraft takes off somewhere in the world and is on schedule 99.96 percent of the time. The fleet's 99.96 dispatch reliability rate translates to less than one aircraft being delayed or canceled for engine-caused reasons upon departure per 2,500 flights. The CFM56 shop visit rate of .075 is equivalent to one unscheduled, engine-caused shop visit every 13,300 hours, and the in-flight shutdown (IFSD) rate of .003 translates to one incident every 333,333 flight hours. On average, an engine in this thrust class would accumulate 2,500 to 3,500 flight hours annually" [26]

It further mentions, "A CFM56-3 engine powering the 737-300 aircraft had already set a record time on wing of 26,000 flight hours without a shop visit with it likely to come in for it only after clocking 30,000 flight hours. Fleet wide, the average time to first shop visit in 1995 was more than 12,300 hours and 9,100 cycles. This rate has continually improved, and newer engines are expected to average more than 14,000 hours and 10,000 cycles before their initial shop visit."[26]

These were simply mind boggling numbers and had not been witnessed by the industry ever, prior to this. The CFM56 engine, thus, was almost like a revolution in air travel which seemingly had broken the traditional iron triangle of air transportation, with its extreme reliability, great performance and lowest possible maintenance costs, while also positively impacting the profitability of operators.

CFM56-5B, for instance, had the lowest shop visit rate of any other engine in its class with each shop visit costing almost $300,000[26] less on a comparative basis. By 1996, there were over 7,400[26] CFM56 engines in-service powering almost 2,600[26] aircrafts worldwide with the engine program having clocked 80,000[26] engine flight hours over 53,000[26] cycles.

The view from deep inside the enemy camp, as elaborated by Pratt & Whitney's Jack Connors in his book, is the most accurate & perfect testimony to CFM56's market success, "Most of us did not see either what was unfolding before us in the 22,000-lb thrust class. Neither the CFM56 nor the JT10D were considered certified engines in the early 1970s. Slowly the CFM56 attained certified status, and in addition the costs of certifying the engine on the airplane seemed to be no problem, as it would be for the JT10D. By that time (referring to CFM56 getting picked for the 737-300 as the exclusive engine), the CFM56 had such a head start that nothing could catch it"[6].

The CFM56 engine family, thus, within a decade-plus span, had come a very long way from the confines of obscurity at launch to almost being terminated after half-a-decade of no demand to being a legend of the skies by having become the default engine choice for the next generation of narrow body aircrafts launched & developed from hereupon in the 1980s decade, which was, in many ways, a truly 'transformational' decade, which provided a tremendous boost to air travel, carriers and the commercial aviation industry broadly and that story will be covered in the next two chapters...

Chapter XI

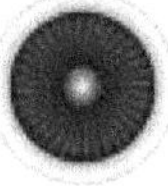

The 'Transformational' Decade' - I

The 1980s was a very different & almost transitional decade given a number of significant changes, market developments and winds of change sweeping across the global commercial aircraft market through the course of the decade. Some of the key, disruptive developments that took place, included:-

1. The Age of Twin-Jets

The most significant change of the 1980s decade was the aviation market's effective transition from the erstwhile era of tri and quad jets to the age of twin jets, not as the exception but rather as the norm, and it was made possible, primarily & collectively, by the increasing reliability of the modern turbofan engines and the unexpected shock of the oil crisis in the 1970s.

In the initial couple of decades, following the dawn of the jet age, airlines had mostly operated aircrafts featuring multiple engines for two reasons, with the first being, that the initial turbofan engines had limited power output, meaning they were not large or powerful enough to be able to provide enough propulsion and aircrafts, thus, needed multiple engines to provide enough thrust, as a result.

The second reason behind it was the logic of system redundancies with multiple engines acting as a backup for each other, in case one or more of the engines give out mid-flight, as the initial turbofans did not have the kind of extreme reliability as their modern counterparts now have which could have been catastrophic, especially in case of transcontinental flights over oceans.

Certain, routes, thus, were restricted solely for tri-jets and quadjets, till the ETOPS came into play, in the mid-1980s. Further, the oil crisis of the 1970s, too, played its part as it made fuel a precious commodity with fuel prices having witnessed a major surge and airlines scrambling for measures to cut down on their rapidly rising operating costs.

Among leading aircraft manufacturers, Boeing had already introduced the 737, as its narrow body twin jet in the mid-1960s which competed with the DC-9, while in the wide body aircraft market, Airbus had introduced its A300/A310 aircraft family at the onset of the 1970s decade.

However, these twin-jet programs (A300/310) were clearly an exception, rather than being the norm of the day, given that the skies at the time were ruled by the very large, wide body tri or quad-jets, namely, the 747 & DC-10, along with some L-1011s with the A300/310 being the odd ones out in the 1970s.

On the narrow body side, the leading aircraft programs were the DC-8, 707 & 727, all of which were either tri or quad jets, with the 737 & DC-9 being the sole crusaders, with the 737 trailing the DC-9 for most of the 1970s decade and commercially really took-off only from the late 1970s onwards.

However, all of it was set to rapidly change at the very onset of the 1980s decade with all new aircraft programs being launched by the aircraft OEMs turning out to be twinjets, as the standard norm, thanks to the high bypass JT9D, CF6 & RB211 turbofan engines on the wide body side of the market and the CFM56 & JT8D engines on the narrow body side, which had proven their reliability sufficiently by now, given that the engine OEMs had addressed their initial teething troubles after their entry into service.

Among industry OEMs, Boeing was the first one to take the leap of faith, following the launch of its 757 narrow body and the 767 medium wide body aircrafts, both of which, were twin jets and were launched in 1978. The move was spearheaded by the launch of the 757 narrow body aircraft program, meant for short & medium haul domestic operations, as a successor to its former 727 tri-jet, and was to complement the 737 in Boeing's aircraft line-up. The 767, which shared the common glass cockpit with the 757, was launched in the same year and was to complement the larger 747 in Boeing's aircraft portfolio.

Boeing, however, had started out on the 767, known initially as 7X7, in two different configurations with one being a trijet and the other being a twin jet. When Boeing offered both configurations to customers for orders, United picked the twin jet while American selected the trijet configuration for the 7X7. However, it was Boeing's legendary designer, Ed Wells (Edward Curtiss Wells); better known by his nickname "the elder statesman of aviation", who had been the company's vice president and a member of the Boeing's board of directors; who had been working behind the scenes post his retirement in 1972 (after having played a pivotal role in designing the 707, 747 and the B-17 Flying Fortress aircrafts), as a consultant to the company at the time, who swayed Boeing's final decision to produce the 767 as a twin jet ultimately.

By the 1980s, Airbus-Boeing rivalry had been duly established and Airbus replied to Boeing's moves, of launching the 757 & 767, with the launch of A330, another twin-jet, and the larger A340, which surprisingly, was a quad-jet powered by 4 CFM56 engines, as Airbus did not duly anticipate the coming ETOPS guidelines for twin-jet operations. Airbus' this decision of developing the A340 as a quad-jet, effectively became the program's 'Achilles Heel', which significantly impeded its ability to compete effectively with Boeing's wide body twin-jets on operating costs going forward.

On the narrow body side of the market, McDonnell Douglas launched and introduced its MD-80, a second-generation derivative of the DC-9 aircraft family in the late 1970s, with a higher MTOW and larger wing, which effectively gave a new lease of life to the original DC-9. The MD-80 was powered by two aft- mounted Pratt & Whitney JT8D-200 high bypass turbofan engines.

Boeing effectively followed up on the 737 Original, comprising 737-100 & 737-200, and decided to further up-the-ante in the narrow body market on arch-rival McDonnell Douglas, by building up on the success of the 737-200 Advanced and announced the development of the 737 Classic series in the late 1970s. The 737 Classic exclusively featured the CFM56 engines, in order, to compete effectively with the MD-80s which were powered by the JT8D-200 series engines. The first variant of the series, 737-300, entered service in 1984.

The 737 Classic, however, also went up against the A320, as Airbus effectively had disrupted the narrow body market in the early 1980s, with its launch of the A320 aircraft family featuring the world's first fly-by-wire controls along with flight envelope protection and CFM56 engines which posed a serious challenge to the 737.

The writing on the wall, thus, was clear that the era of tri and quad jets was effectively over despite the oil prices having plummeted to rock bottom levels in the 1980s and operators were transitioning towards twin jets en-masse, both in the narrow as well as wide body jet segments.

1. De-Regulation of the U.S. Commercial Aviation Market

Commercial aviation in the U.S. was a highly regulated market, until its deregulation by the U.S. Government in 1978, following the enactment of the Airline Deregulation Act by the Congress, which was duly authorized & signed into law by the U.S. President, Jimmy Carter, in October 1978. The passing of the act was primarily intended at fostering & inducing more competition into the market as the government wanted key aspects, especially fares, routes and market players, to be determined by market forces based on free market principles of demand & supply and competition which were so far being carefully controlled & regulated by the Civil Aeronautics Board (CAB).

The deregulation also wanted to prevent industry concentration, which could have led to pursuit of unfair practices by the dominant airlines, while simultaneously encouraging entry of newer market players into the air transportation services market and diversification of existing players across market segments. The act also stated 'the strengthening of small air carriers' as one of its key goals.

The passing of the act effectively removed U.S. Federal government's control over airlines and ushered in the era of free market in the U.S. commercial airline industry marked by a significant increase in the number of flights & miles flown, routes, number of passengers flown & market players while simultaneously leading to a reduction in fares courtesy the efficiencies brought in by the competitive market forces. However, FAA's hawkish control over aviation safety was kept intact even after the passing of the act for the safety of flying passengers.

The act almost caused a tectonic shift in the landscape of the U.S. commercial airline industry which witnessed significant market expansion, air traffic growth and foray of newer players, especially start-ups, and the onset of the era of Low-Cost Carriers (LCCs), which drastically reduced ticket fares and made it effectively possible for the common man to fly which had hitherto been a luxury reserved largely for the wealthy.

The flying public, thus, was the biggest beneficiary of the deregulation move with Economist, Alfred Kahn, estimating that "air fares post market deregulation have lowered by almost 10% to 18% on average as compared to the regulated era with savings to travelers estimated to be in the range of $5 billion to $10 billion annually"[22]

Deregulation and the Airline Industry

However, the overall impact of deregulation on the U.S. airline industry could be termed as, mixed at best, given that the market shares across major carriers had come down significantly following market fragmentation along with average yield as ticket prices went down, thereby, putting pressure on airlines to reduce their cost base.

The active pursuit of cost cutting & austerity measures, geared towards operational efficiencies, led to conflicts & disputes with labor unions which were used to operating with the pre-deregulation ways. Further, deregulation enabled airlines to offer vacant seats on heavy discounts during low demand phases or uptakes, following decontrol of prices, which would have otherwise ended up being lost revenues in the regulated era.

The operational freedom provided by market deregulation enabled major airlines to quickly take business decisions oriented around operational efficiencies. For instance, American Airlines, following deregulation, quickly changed its operating model by adopting the hub-and-spoke model in 1981, after having moved its headquarters from New York to Forth Worth, Texas earlier in 1979, which led to a significant increase in overall efficiencies by aligning aircraft types to route densities with larger jets effectively getting deployed on denser routes while smaller aircrafts deployed in thinner routes.

The Fort Worth International Airport in Dallas, thus, became American's first hub followed by the establishment of the second hub in Chicago, a year later. American also started its Dallas-London transatlantic flight service in 1982 which was followed up by start of international flights to other key European destinations and Japan through the 1980s decade. American also increased its service from 50[22] airports in 1979 to 173[22] airports by 1988 while United grew its services network from 80[22] airports to 169[22] airports over the same period.

Carriers were also able to effectively increase the number of seats on offer in their aircrafts with estimates by economist Alfred Kahn indicating that "airline seating capacity effectively increased by 12% from 136.9 seats on average in 1977 to 153.1 seats by 1988 with carriers also able to fill them more effectively using discounts and offers with flight occupancy growing from 52.6% in the 1968-1978 period up to 61% in the 1978-1990 period"[22]

However, there were also carriers who were simply unable to restructure & align their overall cost base, operational structures and strategies successfully with the new, fundamentally altered market landscape and ultimately succumbed & vanished, filed for bankruptcies or simply got acquired in the post-deregulation industry consolidation phase, ruled by the brutal market forces. The list of such airlines, included, Pan Am, Capitol, Eastern, Continental, American West and TWA.

The deregulation chapter in the U.S. commercial aviation history, thus, was an epoch which effectively took masses up into the skies while, simultaneous, also bringing a number of carriers down to the ground with a thud, who were simply pulled down by the altered rules of the aerial game...

1. Launch of the Airbus' A320 Program

Airbus had been desperately trying to make inroads into the U.S. market, since the launch of the A300/310 wide body aircrafts in the early 1970s, without much success. Airbus, in fact, had been maintaining an inventory of almost two dozen completely built but unused A300 aircrafts at its Toulouse plant in September 1984 amid softening of the overall market demand and given the fact that the airlines were really hesitant to bet on a relatively unknown European player who had just appeared from nowhere, especially on its wide body jet with a substantial price tag. The only major breakthrough Airbus had in the U.S. market, so far (since the launch of A300/310), was the deal signed with Eastern Airlines in 1982 for procurement of 34 A300 aircrafts.

Airbus, thus, decided to penetrate the narrow body aircraft market which was looking really promising after the U.S. market regulation in 1978. Secondly, the availability of the CFM56 high bypass turbofan engine made it even more appealing for Airbus to launch the A320 in the early 1980s featuring an unbeatable combo of innovative technologies packed to the brim and powered by the CFM56 engines.

The technologically superior A320, thus, started gaining deeper roots in the commercial aviation market through the 1980s decade following the initial launch ride provided by the European carriers. Piggybacking on them, it ultimately succeeded in on-boarding many airline customers & operators on-board, even beyond Europe, especially in the U.S. market, leveraging its significant fuel efficiency advantages, emanating from the CFM56-5 series engines over the in-service fleet of 727-200 trijets, DC-9s and MD-80s, which were all powered by Pratt & Whitney's low bypass JT8D engines. Add to that the larger seating capacity & way longer operating range and the A320 clearly had an unbeatable value proposition and almost an overmatch, even over the 737-400.

Airbus, thus, clearly had a narrow body aircraft which could outdo & beat the Boeing's 737 Classic series on a comparative basis, which combined with the radical sales playbook of its master salesman John Leahy, made the overall proposition even more attractive for the airlines and effectively enabled Airbus to make a beachhead in the U.S. market through the 1980s which could subsequently be used to launch a deeper market invasion in the 1990s.

Boeing's demise of the 7J7 program, at the drawing board stage itself, in the second half of 1980s and a delayed decision to launch the 737NG in the early 1990s, provided the perfect launch conditions & runway for the A320 to become airborne and this was precisely the moment in time & history, which marked the onset of a shift in the gravity & strategic calculus of the global narrow body aircraft market from North America towards Europe from the supply side perspective while Boeing leaned towards wide-bodies.

The commercial aircraft market, thus, after a long time, had a third industry OEM making a market foray, after Lockheed's exit from the commercial aviation market post the commercial failure of its L-1011. Airbus' market entry effectively set the stage for the onset of an intense & bitter Trans-Atlantic rivalry, which was going to be fought intensely and in a no-holds-barred manner, over the subsequent decades.

1. Onset of the Airbus-Boeing Rivalry

The keel for the creation & onset of Airbus-Boeing rivalry in the commercial aircraft market had effectively been laid following the introduction of A300/310 by Airbus in the early 1970s. However, it took almost a decade for it to transform into a full-blown war for market shares in the 1980s spearheaded by the narrow body aircraft market.

It had officially begun in the early to mid-1980s, following the launch of the Airbus' A320, which effectively took on the Boeing's second generation of 737, designated as the 737 Classic, and reached its zenith in the 1990s underscored by multiple, hard fought aircraft deals. In the battle for the narrow body market supremacy, the A320 built its sales pitch around its advanced, Fly-by-Wire technology along with significantly lower fuel burn rate & better operating economics, based on its CFM56/V2500 engines, in a direct face-off with the 737-300 as well as the MD-80.

Airbus also claimed that with a long & thin wing, which also had a better aspect ratio, the A320 offered better aerodynamic efficiency than the competing 737 and the MD-80. Boeing had initially ignored the emergence of Airbus and allowed it to create the initial market foothold it had desperately been looking for. Airbus, thus, kept chipping away at Boeing's market share consistently with some hard fought market wins and ultimately toppled McDonnell Douglas to become the second largest market force in commercial aviation. By the turn of the century, Airbus had ultimately had achieved parity with Boeing in terms of market shares.

Boeing, however, reacted strongly to the Airbus' invasion & breach of market sovereignty much later in the mid-1990s and tried to contain Airbus by mounting an unsuccessful counterattack as well but it was all too late by then. Boeing's reactivity in the narrow body market, thus, effectively laid the foundations for the establishment of a well-sustained market duopoly in the commercial aircraft market after the ultimate acquisition of McDonnell Douglas by Boeing in 1997...

Chapter XII

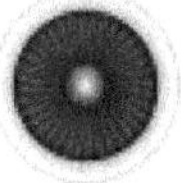

The 'Transformational' Decade - II

1. Extended-Range Twin-Engine Operations Standards or ETOPS Regulations

ETOPS, as an acronym, was coined by the ICAO and simply defines operating standards for twin engine aircrafts, flying on routes over water or remote areas over land, entailing a point on their pre-planned flight path which would be beyond an hour's flying distance from the nearest airport in case one of the two engines becomes inoperative. The logic behind the guideline is built around the risk and the reliability level of engines to ensure that even in case of risky scenarios when one of the engines gives out due to any reason the aircraft should be able to fly on a single engine for more than an hour and reach the nearest airport. Such routes were deemed as risky at the dawn of jet age as well as during the early years and were solely restricted for three and four engine jets as the reliability of early generation, low bypass turbofan engines was deemed inadequate to undertake them.

FAA's 60-Minutes Rule

The rule of 100 miles flying distance to reach an alternate airport for landing, while flying on a single engine, was originally created by the FAA in 1936 under FAR section 121.161 and was applicable to all types of aircrafts irrespective of the engines given the low reliability of piston engines available at the time. The FAA subsequently created the '60-minute' flying time rule to an alternate airport in 1953 and it was intended, primarily, at piston engine-powered commercial aircrafts operating during the 1940s and the early 1950s. However, there was also a provision for the extension of the 60-minute flying time rule based on procurement of regulatory approvals. The ETOPS guidelines, thus, were intended at opening restricted routes for twin-jet operations while maintaining high levels of safety intact.

ICAO's 90-Minutes Guideline

The ICAO, in the meanwhile, proposed its more flexible 90-minute diversion time rule in 1953, which was applicable to all aircrafts. It was accepted by many non-U.S. based aviation regulators and effectively enabled non-U.S. carriers to use their twins on routes which were typically & solely restricted for tri and quad jets only under the old rules. The guideline was based on data & statistics which revealed that jet engines were almost 10 times[23] more reliable than their piston engine counterparts, statistically. The FAA, however, stuck to its strict 60-minutes flying time mandate.

ICAO's ETOPS Rule Update in the 1980s

The ETOPS rules were again updated by the ICAO in the early 1980s, under its new ICAO study group, in collaboration with the respective civil aviation regulatory authorities across nations while taking effective cognizance of the much higher reliability of jet engines. Also, it had been duly established that the increase in size as well as power output of jet engines did not have any impact on their reliability levels.

Further, technological advancements brought in by the availability of latest performance standards and safety features in commercial aircrafts now created enhanced safety levels for aviation in the 1980s. ETOPS regulations, thus, were relaxed and amended in light of availability of these new, advanced twin-jets powered by highly reliable turbofans with the creation of ICAO's Annex 6 which recommended 120- minutes ETOPS for these aircrafts meeting advanced safety criteria, intended primarily at the commercially attractive & highly competitive North Atlantic routes which would have benefitted tremendously with twin-jet operations, while keeping all other turbofan-powered older twins to 60 minutes flying time.

FAA's 120-Minutes ETOPS Guideline

In 1985, the FAA created fresh ETOPS guidelines under its FAR 121.161, thereby, approving 120- minutes flying time deviation for twins. Following FAA, many other aviation regulators across most key markets issued their ETOPS guidelines as well which were based on ICAO's Annex 6. Overall satisfactory operational experience with the 120-minutes ETOPS eventually led to the push for the 180- minutes ETOPS by the industry, which would have been a game changer given that it would have enabled carriers to virtually fly almost any route globally using twins.

FAA's 180-Minutes ETOPS Guideline

FAA subsequently approved the 180-minutes ETOPS criteria for twin jets in January 1989 under its AC 120-42"A", based on incorporation of major design enhancements as well as the high reliability of high bypass turbofans, which cleared the runway for twin-jets to undertake intercontinental flights covering almost every possible route on the planet. It, thus, came as a major victory for twin-jets and boost for the carriers.

The ETOPS criteria were crucial for carriers, especially with their ongoing gradual liberalization over the course of the 1980s decade. It almost coincided with the end of Cold War, which effectively unleashed the era of globalization at the turn of the decade, and which had these long distance twin-jets, efficiently connecting continents seamlessly, as its true backbone.

These new ETOPS criteria also enabled the creation of large, next generation wide bodies in the 1990s decade by both Airbus and Boeing which were looking for ways to effectively ride the tailwinds of change...

1. **Great Engine Wars in Military Aviation – GE vs. Pratt & Whitney**

In the 1980s, the raging Cold War between the United States and the U.S.S.R. was at its peak following the invasion of Afghanistan by the Soviet forces in 1979. However, another war was being waged within the United States and it was between GE Aviation and Pratt & Whitney respectively. Termed as the 'Great Engine War', it was geared towards & was a relentless quest for supremacy of the U.S. military aircraft engines market.

The United States, following significant air combat losses recorded during the Vietnam War, had been updating its air war doctrine comprehensively which accompanied the development of new & next generation fighter jets, incorporating learning & inputs from the Vietnam war theater as well as fighter pilots who had served there. The changes were also being made in view of the development of new fighter jets by the Soviet Union, especially the Su-27

'Flanker' (NATO designation) family of heavy fighter jets at the top end of the spectrum and the more maneuverable MiG-29 'Fulcrum' (NATO designation) at the lower end.

The U.S. had responded to these advanced aerial moves by its arch-rival by having developed its own F-14 Tomcat developed by Grumman Corporation, as the supersonic aerial interceptor to be operated by the U.S. Navy in 1972 (EIS), featuring the swing-wing and powered by the Pratt & Whitney's TF-30 engines. It was followed up by the development of the F-15 Eagle (developed in parallel with the F-14) by McDonnell Douglas Corporation for the U.S. Air Force as its top-end jet, primarily, for Aerial Interception and Air-to-Air combat roles.

The F-15 Eagle was to be accompanied by the highly maneuverable F-16 Fighting Falcon as the air superiority and multirole fighter at the lower end of the spectrum and was also being developed for exports to the NATO allies. The Department of Defense awarded the development contract for the F-16 in the mid-1970s to General Dynamics Corporation. Both the F-15 and the F-16 were to be produced in huge numbers and were to be the backbone of the U.S. Air Force and NATO allies for a long time given the traditional, long life spans of fighter jets of almost 3-4 decades.

The 'Great Engine Wars', waged between GE Aviation and Pratt & Whitney, were essentially for the development of the 'best' engines for the F-15 and F-16 fighter jet programs and to capture the largest share of the engines contracts being awarded by the Department of Defense (DOD) through the 1970s, 1980s and through to the very end of the Cold War worth billions of dollars.

Pratt & Whitney had developed its F100 engine for the twin-engine powered, F-15 Eagle, while its arch-rival, GE Aviation, had developed the F110 for the same (excluding the multiple engine variants, featuring different thrust classes, developed by them for international variants of the F-15 Eagle program like the F-15K for South Korea, F-15J for Japan and the F-15SA for Saudi Arabia).Interestingly, the F110 was derived from the F101, which powered the Rockwell B-1 Lancer, and was quintessentially another variant of the 'GE1' building block.

The U.S. Navy and the USAF had originally issued the RFPs jointly for the development & procurement of engines for the F-14 & the F-15 programs, under its Interim Engine Development Program (IEDP) in 1967, with Pratt & Whitney and GE Aviation being the two final downselects in the high stakes program. In 1970, Pratt & Whitney's F100 engine was selected as the winner of the contest and the F100-PW-100 ultimately powered the F-15 Eagle's initial variants. The single engine F-16 program, too, entered service powered by the F100-PW-200, a variant of the -100, with better reliability and reduced engine stall rates. This was a resounding, early victory for Pratt & Whitney, against arch-rival GE Aviation, in the military aviation propulsion market.

The Pratt & Whitney's F100-PW-100/200, however, had reliability, maintenance & durability issues and given the USAF's need for additional power output for its tactical aircrafts; the USAF officials sought improvements from Pratt & Whitney while also funding the development of an alternate engine, under its Alternate Fighter Engine (AFE) program (in form of the GE's F110). It was geared towards invoking forces of competition, for best results as well as output, which is a common practice in defense programs and it effectively marked the onset of the 'Great Engine Wars' between the incumbent Pratt & Whitney and the challenger GE Aviation.

Pratt & Whitney replied with an improved F100-PW-229 while GE fought its way back into the fray, with its F110-GE-129 engine in the 1980s, thereby, officially unleashing the subsequent rounds of the intense rivalry between the two American engine powerhouses to play out in the marketplace for winning engine contracts for different aircraft production 'Blocks' from the USAF for the F-15s & F-16s (from thereupon) with both the engines ultimately powering different blocks of the F-15 & F-16 programs.

The point to be noted here is that these were massive contracts worth billions of dollars for the development of highly complex, state-of-the-art military turbofan engines and engaged significant R&D, production and engineering resources at both GE Aviation as well as Pratt & Whitney while they were slugging it out on the commercial side of the aviation market as well.

It, thus, duly had an impact on their overall ability regarding pursuit of new engine programs as well as development of cutting edge technologies, in view of the potential resource constraints imposed by the two-front war between the arch-rivals, which is an important perspective to be factored in, while analyzing the overall scheme of things and taking an overarching view of the overall battle theater, including, both military and commercial sides of the aviation market.

Interestingly, the same script is being re-enacted with history duly repeating itself almost 4 decades later in the 2020s now, on the even bigger F-35 program, with the incumbent, Pratt & Whitney, as the sole engine provider (with its F-135 engine) effectively blocking & resisting GE Aviation's indirect entry on to the program, as the alternate engine provider with its sixth generation adaptive cycle engine, the XA-100, while Pratt & Whitney is actively promoting further engine core upgrades on the F-135 engine, as the best pathway forward, towards meeting greater power and additional cooling requirements for the F-135 engine.

It will be really interesting to see as to how the incessant power plays between the arch-rivals and the almost fabled rivalry play out this time around...

Chapter XIII

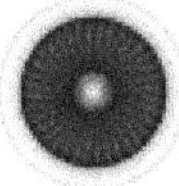

The 'Uncharted' Flight Path

The U.S. economy effectively entered recession in July 1980, as a fallout of the Fed's efforts to combat rising inflation levels with monetary policy tightening, which led to a surge in unemployment rate, which went up to 7.5%. The developing situation, however, was a culmination of the 'Stop-Go' monetary policy stance adopted by the Fed through the 1960s & the 1970s decades, as discussed earlier. The Fed operated under the premise that it could actually lower the unemployment rate while keeping inflation at manageable levels, under a trade-off conventionally referred to as the 'Phillips Curve'. The Fed's policy was reactive and alternated between periods of interest rates lowering to address unemployment levels and raising interest rates to contain inflation when it crossed the manageable threshold.

The policy, however, ultimately failed, while proving to be unstable and unsustainable, as by the mid-1970s the unemployment levels and inflation rates both rose simultaneously. Inflation, thus, was standing at 11%[36] by 1979 and the Fed this time initiated a determined fight against inflation, under the command of Paul Volcker as the Fed Chair appointed in August 1979. The Fed's overarching focus & stance was a persistent monetary policy tightening, with a firm foot on the brakes, till complete victory was achieved. By 1981, the federal funds rate was soaring at 20%[36] while the ten-year Treasury bond rate had surged from 10% in 1980 to 15%[36] within a year.

By the late 1982, the unemployment rate was at its highest level observed since the World War II, after the U.S. economy had officially entered recession in the third quarter of 1981. However, despite mounting pressure to reduce rates Volcker refused to budge and by October 1982, inflation had been fully crushed and contained as it came down to just 5%[36] marking a key victory for Fed and the U.S. economy. However, in term of the broader industry impact; manufacturing, construction and the auto industries were the usual victims and were most impacted by this downturn phase with goods producers collectively having accounted for almost 90% of the total job losses in the year 1982 alone.

In terms of commercial aviation, this was the phase when the industry had to pursue measures to actively reduce aircraft noise, following the Congress' enactment of the noise reduction act in 1978 which had a compliance window of up to 1983. The airlines, thus, were in the process of either buying hush kits for their older aircrafts or re-engining them with newer, low-noise engines as simply recapitalizing their old fleets was the most difficult option during this phase with interest rates almost skyrocketing. Further, following deregulation, the air traffic numbers had started zooming up and the airlines' new found strategic autonomy enabled them to manage their operations in the most efficient manner by aligning routes with aircraft deployments optimally.

The supply side of the industry, however, was busy, active & fully engaged during this phase with the development of new products and technologies to power the future of commercial aviation. Boeing had already announced its next generation 737 Classic, comprising the 737-300 & -400, featuring the new CFM56-3 engines. Boeing had also launched its new 757 aircraft program, as a replacement for its 727 along with the 767 medium, wide body jet, with both being almost on the verge of market entry in the early 1980s and spearheaded the market's transition towards twin jets.

Airbus, too, had started penetrating the U.S. commercial aircraft market slightly with its A300/310 programs while still actively seeking a substantial breakthrough. United and Delta were getting their old DC-8s re-engined with the new CFM56 engines. McDonnell Douglas had already launched the second generation of its DC-9, in form of the MD-80 series, while Airbus was gearing up to launch its A320 aircraft program.

For engine OEMs, too, it was an active & busy time, especially for CFM International and particularly for its CFM56 program, whose time for deliverance & redemption had finally arrived. GE Aviation was busy refining & tidying up its CF6 engine program, through the development of CF6-80 engine series (which included the CF6-80A & CF6-80C2) to power the new as well as existing wide body aircraft programs which were being launched by the aircraft OEMs.

Pratt & Whitney had its JT8D-200 series engines entering service powering the McDonnell Douglas' MD-80 series in 1980 while it was also leading a pack of engine manufacturers in the early 1980s and laying the ground work for the creation of an engine alliance behind the scenes, in order, to compete effectively with the CFM56 engine.

The Road Leading Up to the JT10D and the PW2000 Series Ultimately

In the early 1970s, the USAF expressed the requirement for a jet powered military transport aircraft with a short take-off and landing capability following which the ROC & RFI were duly floated under the Advanced Medium STOL Transport (AMST) program. Boeing (with its YC-14) and McDonnell Douglas (with its YC-15) were the two final downselects in the competition. The USAF had also launched the Advanced Turbine Engine (ATE) program alongside to power the AMST. It was to be a 23,000 lbf class high bypass turbofan engine for which Pratt & Whitney had duly submitted the proposal.

However, owing to a funding crunch for R&D, the ATE engine program was axed by the USAF while the AMST was retained. The AMST prototype was ultimately tested powered by both JT8D-219 as well as the CFM56 engines. Pratt & Whitney's internal team of engineers, however, kept working on the experimental engine which was to be developed under the ATE program and got it to a working engine stage as a technology demonstrator and designated it as the JT10D.

Pratt & Whitney actively sought international collaborations for taking the JT10D further, in order to share the technical & financial risks involved, while also opening the international market (primarily Europe) for the engine. Pratt & Whitney was able to line-up MTU, Fiat & Alfa Romeo for the program and later even got Rolls Royce to participate in it to develop a family of medium thrust commercial engines with power output ranging from 25,000 to 30,000 lbf.

Pratt & Whitney's internal market assessments and long range planning, as early as 1971, had projected the strong rise of the 25,000-30,000 lbf thrust class engine, as per Jack Connors.[6] However, lack of any tangible commercial aircraft requirements at the time (which could have justified outpouring of billions of dollars into a new engine program altogether) led to squandering of the opportunity effectively by Pratt & Whitney.

The JT10D development entailed a number of radical approaches to turbofan engine design aimed at increasing fuel efficiency, which included, a reduction in the number of parts, a higher bypass ratio, increased overall pressure ratio and for the first time in commercial aviation history, the usage of a full authority digital electronic control (FADEC), which effectively replaced the cables running from aircraft engines to the cockpit. In 1982, Pratt & Whitney adopted a new engine naming convention (mentioned a little later in this chapter) under which the JT10D was re-designated as the PW2000 with a thrust class ranging from 20,000 to 30,000 lbf.

Boeing had been developing its next generation of airplanes for the 1980s decade, as a family of aircrafts (designated internally as the 7N7 & 7X7), which were launched in 1978 and ultimately turned out to be 757 and 767 respectively. The 757 narrow body aircraft was a replacement for the 727-200 but Boeing needed a super fuel efficient engine for it after the oil crisis. Pratt & Whitney instantly recognized the moment of reckoning for its JT10D and offered the engine while designating it as the PW2037.

Ironically, following the outlining of the engine requirement for the 7N7 program, Rolls Royce & Pratt & Whitney were once again found standing on the opposite sides of the fence in the battle for the 7N7, as Rolls Royce, too, had pitched its own derivative engine for it.

GE, however, decided to stay away from the competition as it determined that the potential market size for this kind of an engine being too small to justify committing billions towards new engine development. The eventual turn of events, as they turned out over the course of time, aptly proved that GE, indeed, was right in its judgment. Pratt & Whitney, too, was consciously aware of it but gave it a go as it was "the only game in town"[6] as Jack Connors has put it in his book.

The 757 program, thus, was ultimately won by Pratt & Whitney with its PW2037 which had a bypass ratio of 6:1 and a thrust output range of 38,400 lbf to 43,734 lbf. However, for the 757, the PW207 was to generate 37,000 lbf of thrust and was ultimately launched by Pratt & Whitney in December 1979, along with MTU and Fiat as industrial partners, which owned 11% and 4% stakes in the engine program respectively. The PW2037 also became the first commercial engine in aviation history to feature FADEC which is a standard now on all engines.

The PW2037 was also selected by the USAF for its C-17 military transport aircraft subsequently, as the culmination of the AMST program of the early 1970s, announced in August 1981, which was to be produced by McDonnell Douglas, based on its YC-15 proposal, sporting 4 PW2037 engines with a slightly higher thrust rating than the commercial variant used on the 757.

The Emergence of the PW4000 Series

Pratt & Whitney, however, had another card up its sleeve and the company had secretly been playing it behind the scenes. It was the development of a new, scratch up engine family, targeted at the wide body aircrafts, based on technology which the company had developed for the JT10D but at a bigger scale for wide body applications.

Pratt & Whitney's internal market assessment, released to media in a company presentation made in December 1982, pegged the total market for new engines over the 1982-1992 decade at almost 6,000[37] units worth $25[37] billion. This brand new, wide body engine family was collectively termed by Pratt & Whitney as the PW4000 series and had, lower operating economics and advanced technology, as its two key differentiators.

Pratt & Whitney announced the new engine family (with the company planning to cover a thrust output range of up to 100,000 lbf.) in a media presentation, which was covered prominently by The New York Times in a story[37] published on December 1982, which reported that the new PW4000 engine family was to focus on the 48,000 to 60,000 lbf thrust output range and was to effectively succeed the JT9D engine program while featuring a

54%[37] reduction in the number of parts (translating into 27,000 fewer parts than the JT9D) and delivering a 7%[37] better operating economics for the airlines.

The first development engine program from the PW4000 series was the PW4052 which was going to have a thrust output range of 52,000 lbf and was going to be for a Boeing program. Further, as per the new engine designation nomenclature unveiled by Pratt & Whitney from 1981 onwards for the PW4000 series engines, the last two digits of the engine number (for instance PW4052) indicated the thrust output (52,000 lbf for PW4052) while the digit '0' before that indicated that it is for Boeing's wide body aircraft programs, namely, 767, 747 or 777, whereas, digit '1' here denoted Airbus aircraft programs, namely, A300/310 & the A330. The digit '4' in the middle indicated McDonnell Douglas' MD-11 program.

It, however, may not have been an easy decision for Pratt & Whitney to make a clear departure away from the JT9D, the engine for which Pratt & Whitney had even won the Collier Trophy in 1970, just a decade ago. However, the market forces demanded it given that the market was moving towards twin jets weighing up to 500,000 lb. which were invariably going to be powered by just two large, powerful and reliable engines generating thrust output of up to 100,000 lbf (each engine) over long term.

The emerging market trend, thus, would have effectively meant the end of the road for the JT9D program whose largest variant, JT9D-7R4H1 produced for the A300-600 in July 1982, had a peak thrust output of 56,000 lbf, as compared to the top variant of the GE Aviation's CF6-80 series, which peaked out at 72,000 lbf.

Further, developing a new engine from scratch is the difficult pathway fraught with a multitude of serious technology and financial risks, including, potential engine recalls, provision for spare engines, warranty expenses, in addition, to unpleasant lawsuits & financial claims leading up to compensation payout scenarios to operators, in case of inability of the engine to meet or its non-adherence with the performance standards promised initially.

The derivative strategy of developing engine variants, thus, is relatively a much safer and way more cost effective strategy than putting huge sums into the development of altogether new, scratch-up programs, getting them certified and then getting through the long, grinding & arduous process of fine- tuning them through the initial teething troubles over their early, difficult years of service.

It further becomes, even more of a financial ordeal, given the traditional operating model followed by the industry in which commercial engines usually are sold almost at a loss to airlines and the engine makers subsequently recoup their huge invested sums largely from maintenance, repair & overhaul (MRO) activity of these engines which usually comes only after the engines have accumulated years worth of flight hours.

Pratt & Whitney's primary drive behind pursuing this risk fraught strategy of going with a completely new engine was to be future-ready while being a step ahead of its existing market competitors, namely, arch-rival GE Aviation's CF6 and Rolls Royce's RB211 engine programs, in terms, of technology as well as operating economics.

The focus clearly was a quest for one-upmanship along with a much larger share of the large turbofan engines market with radical innovation as the core pivot. The NYT article[37] (cited above as well) further unravels that Pratt & Whitney's plan to achieve 54% parts reduction was centered on the company's transition to engines with higher rotation speeds. The author wrote, "How does the company plan to produce its engine with 54 percent, or 27,000, fewer parts than in its best existing engine? A brochure explained that the new engine would operate at higher rotation speeds. Higher rotation, it said, made it possible to use 12 percent fewer fan blades, 30 percent fewer compressor blades, and 50 percent fewer high-pressure turbine blades. The brochure also attributed the parts reduction to greater simplicity in design and construction techniques".[37]

Pratt & Whitney's grand plan was to replace the JT9D engine with a family of new wide-body class engines with thrust output ranging from 50,000 lbf to 100,000 lbf while the primary challenge it faced was achieving it without getting the company into a financial mess, ultimately driving it towards bankruptcy, given the scale of investments involved.

The plan entailed developing a common, large engine core and subsequently developing & carving three scaled variants out of it. These engine variants were to operate with three different spools and to be equipped with fans of three different sizes while fully leveraging commonality among engine parts, components as well as tooling while ensuring reliability, performance and scaled growth in thrust output and containing overall risks.

The industry experts, however, were skeptic at best and disbelieving at worst over Pratt & Whitney's move given that the trio of Pratt & Whitney, GE Aviation and Rolls Royce were almost equal rivals in terms of technological prowess & capabilities and there was or could be no clear winner which could have unanimously been awarded the heavyweight title for market hegemony, dominance & leadership and the industry watchers & experts were unanimous in this verdict of theirs.

While Pratt & Whitney was effectively moving forward with its PW4000 series bet worth billions of dollars announced in late 1982; GE Aviation was developing a new variant of its CF6 engine, termed as the CF6-80 series for the 1980s decade, featuring a thrust output increase to up to 62,000 lbf. The engine prototype had already produced 61,000 lbf of thrust in its initial tests conducted in June 1981 while Rolls Royce had actively been working towards increasing the thrust output of its RB211 engine to match GE Aviation, in almost a toe-to-toe contest. GE Aviation's CF6-80 series, thus, was scheduled to be certified at least a year ahead of Pratt & Whitney's PW4000 series and was poised to start its commercial market campaign with a virtual head start over its traditional arch-rival.

When Robert J. Carlson, United Technologies' executive vice president, who had briefed reporters in the company presentation to media in December 1982, was quizzed whether Pratt & Whitney (with its PW4000 series launch) was playing a catch-up game to gain a larger share of the market pie for large turbofan engines, in the three way competition with GE & Rolls Royce after the recession was over, he had replied, "It's the other way around, by a substantial amount,"[37]

Mr. Carlson further said, "He understood that the new General Electric engine was based on those currently in use"[37]. By contrast, he contended, Pratt & Whitney was starting with "a clean sheet of paper'[37]' and "would provide economies far beyond what its competitor was talking about"[37]. However, in reality, Pratt & Whitney was way behind in development schedule when compared to GE Aviation, as Pratt did not even have a fully assembled engine prototype to test while GE had already tested its CF6-80 series more than a year-and-a-half ago. Secondly, GE's CF6-80 series was a derivative engine based on the proven CF6 engine program while the PW4000 series was being built from scratch. GE Aviation, thus, clearly had an upper hand here over Pratt & Whitney, at least, in overall risk levels & development schedule aspects.

GE Aviation's CF6-80 series of new generation turbofans covered a thrust output range of 48,000 lbf to 75,000 lbf with the first member of the family, the CF6-80A, featuring a thrust output range of 48,000 lbf to 50,000 lbf while entering commercial service to power the Boeing's 767 in 1982 and Airbus' A310 program in 1983 respectively. The CF6-80 series essentially had been derived from the older CF6-50 series, with the duo, sharing almost the same mechanical configuration.

Pratt & Whitney's PW4052, on the contrary, received certification only in 1987 which clearly gave the CF6-80 series a definite & huge head start of almost 3-4 years in a fast & rapidly growing market environment especially after the recession of the early 1980s was over. The PW4000-94 series, with a thrust output range of 50,000 lbf to 62,000 lbf, had a slightly higher bypass ratio (BPR) ranging from 4.8 to 5.1 along with a higher pressure ratio, as compared, to CF6-80A's 4.59 to 4.66 BPR and a peak thrust output of 48,000 to 50,000 lbf.

Further, GE's largest variant of the CF6, the CF6-80E1, had a peak take-off thrust output of almost 70,000 lbf, whereas, the top tier of the PW4000 engine family, the PW4000-112, had a thrust output range of 74,000 lbf to 98,000 lbf.

Pratt & Whitney, thus, had a slight technological overmatch over GE Aviation as GE had a clear void in its large engines line-up and would have had to create a new engine from scratch to match Pratt's top end in the wide body market now.

The third key market force in commercial aviation, Rolls Royce, too, was gearing up for this second round (after the first one through the 1970s decade) of this three-way battle for supremacy of wide body propulsion with the company having just been emancipated from the clutches of regulation and red tape following its privatization in 1987.

Rolls Royce also had outlined plans to chart a similar flight path, just as Pratt & Whitney, in developing a new engine family from scratch, despite the success of its RB211 engine, while retaining the three spool architecture of the RB211 for the new engine family, which was launched initially as the RB-211-524L but was ultimately christened as Trent, after Rolls Royce's tradition & naming convention of naming its engines after the names of rivers in the United Kingdom.

Rolls Royce, however, was one of the last, among the trio of engine makers, to enter the wide body fray in the 1980s decade with the creation of the Trent high bypass turbofan engine family, which was announced only in June 1988, with a thrust output range of 61,900 lbf to 97,000 lbf (almost matching Pratt & Whitney), with the first variant, the Trent 700 undertaking its maiden flight in 1990 and going on to power the A330 way later in 1995.

Rolls Royce's move clearly was slightly behind the waves of market evolution, progression & development from a competitive standpoint and gave significant leeway to rivals, GE Aviation and Pratt & Whitney, to further up their game and consolidate their already strong grip on the wide body aircraft propulsion market. However, it was still, just in time to be meaningful, as the market was rapidly moving towards the 100,000 lbf thrust threshold, and required some serious catch up to be played by Rolls Royce ultimately.

It would be interesting to cover the mechanics & dynamics of the three-way battles for market shares which were waged in the large engines market segment over the course of the 1990s decade and in the 21st century, however, that is only going to be within the purview of the next part of this two-part book series...

Chapter XIV

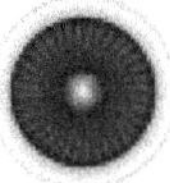

The End of an 'Era'

The dramatic rise of the CFM International's CFM56 program, at the onset of the 1980s decade; following, its selection for re-engining of United and Delta's old DC-8s and for powering the Boeing's 737 Classic aircraft generation as the exclusive power plant; had caused other engine makers to take notice of the developing market dynamic and a likely, potential loss of market shares almost imminent, going forward. It was especially true for Pratt & Whitney which still had its 1960s era, JT8D engine as the bedrock of its medium thrust engines business and especially the narrow body aircraft propulsion market.

A New York Times article, published in 1985, themed on Pratt & Whitney's JT8D engine program, captured the zeitgeist of the time in its true essence while also putting things in perspective for us. Titled "Pratt & Whitney's Workhorse"[24], the article mentions that the JT8D engine accounted for almost a 50% share of the engines (in units) shipped by Pratt & Whitney at the time, "for 1984, Pratt & Whitney shipped 455 jet engines, of which, 250 were JT8Ds"[24]. The article further underscores that the commercial aircraft market in the mid-1980s was on a roll following the deregulation of 1978 (as covered earlier); "The demand for new jet engines and spare parts is expected to exceed $71 billion over the next 10 years, compared with $39 billion in the previous 10 years."[24]

Pratt & Whitney's market position in the narrow body aircraft segment, seemingly, was under serious threat amid a rapidly growing commercial aviation market. However, it was not just because of the rising competition but rather also because of the two, back-to-back, fatal air crashes caused by engine failures of JT8D engines, within a span of weeks, killing 84 people.

A DC-9, powered by the JT8D-15 engines, had crashed in July 1985 (following an engine loss) while a British Air's Boeing 737 crashed within weeks in August 1985 (with its combustor chamber exploding) putting a serious question mark on the JT8D's unmatched reliability and impeccable safety record, since its market entry over two decades ago in 1964.

In fact, the in-flight shutdown rate of the JT8D engine program was 0.02[6] meaning "the need to shutdown an engine mid-flight would only arise once in almost 50,000 flight hours or 17 years"[6] which had almost set a new industry standard for engine reliability. However, in this regard, the CFM56 engine proved to be a step further ahead of the JT8D, with its in-flight engine shutdown rate of 0.003[26], as claimed by CFM International, translating into an in-flight shutdown rate of once in almost 333,333[33] flight hours or almost 100[33] years (given that a commercial engine in the medium thrust class usually flies an average of 3000-4000 flight hours annually).

The industry analysts, however, did not anticipate any fallout on Pratt & Whitney or the JT8D program, even after the twin crashes. A media article captured the views of two key aerospace analysts of the time regarding the impact of crashes. Wolfgang Demish, aerospace analyst for the First Boston Corporation, had remarked, "The impact on the company, I still think, is essentially nil. The engine, over all, has the best reliability record of any jet engine in the country. I believe this, even with the last two accidents factored in."[24] John D. Campbell, aerospace analyst for Goldman, Sachs & Company added, "You are not going to get something on these engines that makes them less airworthy."[24]

The article further mentions, Pratt & Whitney had first found problems with the combustion chamber, following instances of cracks appearing, being reported by the operators. Pratt & Whitney, in fact, had already started informing operators, in the early 1980, about opting for combustion chamber checks, in case, slow engine starts or slow acceleration were experienced. Even the FAA, in 1984, had ordered modifications & new engine inspection procedures on the JT8D-15 variant. The articles closes on a defiant note as far as Pratt & Whitney's overall stance and impact on market positioning was concerned. It categorically said, "Whatever the findings; Pratt & Whitney is not likely to easily yield its position as the top maker of civilian aircraft engines."[24]

The JT8D program and Pratt & Whitney's market shares, in the narrow body market, thus, were on the line and had been on a clearly anticipated, slow decline trajectory following the advent of the high bypass CFM56 engine in the late 1970s and following its selection to power the next generation narrow bodies, namely, Boeing's 737 Classic and Airbus' A320 programs. Pratt & Whitney, however, was not going to easily squander its leading market position in the narrow bodies segment and the company pursued a two-pronged strategy to counter the rise of its highly capable competitor, CFMI & its CFM56 program.

The JT8D-200 Series Engine

Pratt & Whitney had been a participant in NASA's Quiet Engine Program, which spanned from 1972 to 1975, and actively worked towards reducing engine noise, in view, of the significance being placed on active reduction of noise emanating from aircrafts at the time. For the program, Pratt & Whitney's JT8 core was used, along with a new larger fan, translating into an overall higher bypass ratio for the new JT8D-109 (engine designation).

The flight testing of the engine, subsequently, on a DC-9-30 flying test bed, provided promising results which prompted Pratt & Whitney to develop it as an altogether new variant of the JT8D, which formed the basis for the JT8D-200 series, comprising the -217 and -219 engine programs, and had its EIS in 1980.

The JT8D-200 series featured a much larger fan, with the fan diameter increased by almost 10 inches to 54 inches, which along with other minor adjustments & changes, increased its bypass ratio from 0.96:1 for the original JT8D-17/19 to almost 1.78:1[6] (1.74:1 as per MTU[28]) for the JT8D-200 series, translating into a substantial reduction in thrust specific fuel consumption (TSFC) of almost 12%[6] (as compared to the original JT8D) while also leading to an increase in range and overall payload capacity, leading to an increased revenue potential, especially for freighters.

The JT8D-200 also featured the exhaust mixer; which effectively mixed the high velocity, noisier air exhaust from the turbine discharge with the low velocity, low noise air exhaust of the bypass duct; resulting in a slight overall noise reduction of almost 6 dB for the JT8D-200 series.

The JT8D-200 series also had MTU Aero Engines as an industrial and risk-and-revenue sharing partner with a 12.5%[28] ownership share of the program.MTU, thus, was responsible for the development of the low pressure turbine (LPT) apart from manufacture of a range of low pressure turbine (LPT) parts and high pressure compressor (HPC) & turbine parts along with the housing. The JT8D-200 program also had Mitsubishi and GKN Aerospace as program and industrial partners.

In this context, a comparison between the original JT8D-17 and the JT8D-217/219 engines on performance data was done by FedEx, while re-engining its in-service, old 727 freighters with the newer JT8D-217/219 engines under the Super 27 program in the late 1990s. It was reported by Guy Norris (the current propulsion systems editor of the reputed Aviation Week magazine) for the Flight Global magazine, way back in 1999.

FedEx found, post re-engining its 727 workhorses, that their fuel efficiency increased in the range of almost 11%[25] to 14%[25] while payload capacity (crucial for freighters) went up by almost thrice, from 6,800kg earlier to 18,200kg[25], along with a range increase of 300 NM[25] and much better short-field performance.

The JT8D-200 series comprised three engine variants, namely, the JT8D-209, -217 and -219 with their thrust output ranging from 18,500 lbf for the -209 to 21,700 lbf for the -219. The JT8D-200 series received FAA certification in 1979 and entered service, as the exclusive engine on the McDonnell Douglas' MD-80 aircraft series, which essentially was the second generation of its original DC-9 narrow body program.

The MD-80 series was launched in 1977, ultimately entered service in 1980 and comprised 5 aircraft variants, namely, MD-81, MD-82, MD-83, MD-87 and the MD-88. The MD-80 series was the first of the new generation of narrow bodies entering the market in the 1980s decade following market deregulation, giving McDonnell Douglas a clear head start (just like the DC-9

& the DC-8 earlier). The MD-80 also was most competitive in the market, in terms of acquisition costs, and it competed directly with the Boeing's second generation 737 Classic, and later also with the Airbus' A320 program, both of which were powered by the CFM56 engines.

Getting the sole engine position on the MD-80 series provided a new lease of life to the 1960s-era JT8D engine program, of course, in its -200 series avatar, while also opening the re-engining market for older aircrafts. The JT8D-200 may not have been a technological match (and it was not even intended at that) for the technologically way superior CFM56 (in terms of bypass ratio & the thrust specific fuel consumption) which was almost 20% more fuel efficient than the JT8D, way more durable & reliable and clearly being a generational leap rather than just being an incremental shift.

However, in terms of cost, the JT8D-200 was way more competitive than the CFM56 with the list price of a JT8D-200 reported to be around $4 million[25] per engine (in the late1990s) as compared to $5+ million[26] list price for the CFM56-5B (in 2004), owing, primarily, to the 1960s-era technology it contained and courtesy Pratt & Whitney's fully amortized production line for the JT8D.

The move, however, did extend the life span of the JT8D program by almost another 2 decades, while effectively excluding the MRO revenues emanating from the in-service fleet, which would have been sizeable as well given that Delta (the launch customer for the DC-9 in 1965, MD-88 in 1988 and for MD-90 in 1995) only retired its fleet of 47 MD-88s & 29 MD-90s in early 2020, after the onset of COVID-19 pandemic.

Further, as discussed earlier as well, the commercial airline industry works on operating economics rather than just capability addition. Thus, technologically, the relatively inferior MD-80 series (based on the 1960s-era DC-9) powered by the 1960s-era technology, in form of the JT8D-200, did just fine for the airlines, even in the 1980s.

It was so because its acquisition cost was relatively much lower (as compared to the Being 737 Classic generation and the Airbus' A320 program) while complying with all regulatory requirements, including noise, along with the added advantage of low maintenance costs.

McDonnell Douglas, thus, ended up producing and selling almost 1,200 MD-80 series aircrafts (along with 2500+ JT8D-200 series engines powering them, excluding spare engines altogether, worth over $10 billion+ on list prices) from 1979 through to the turn of the century, till McDonnell Douglas ultimately was acquired by Boeing in 1997.

Pratt & Whitney ultimately sold almost 14,750[29] JT8D engines (including the -200 series) which clocked over 673 million[29] flight hours collectively. Pratt & Whitney, later also developed an E-Kit for the JT8D-200 series, which effectively reduced its nitrogen oxide emissions by almost 25%, thereby, ensuring its compliance with the prevailing environmental regulations, in order, to further extend the life of the in-service engines.

The Super 27 Program

The JT8D-200 series engine also enabled the launch of the Super 27 program by the aftermarket players in the late 1980s and the 1990s. The program was aimed at re-engining the older, in-service Boeing 727s with the JT8D-217/ 219 engines which would have enabled these old workhorses to stay airborne by complying with the stringent noise regulations (Stage 3 noise level requirements of the FAA's Part 36 & chapter 3 requirements of the ICAO's Annex 16 which would have needed hush kits for original JT8D engines worth $2.8 million[25]) while also improving fuel efficiency and increasing overall payload capacity.

As mentioned earlier, FedEx found post re-engining its 727 workhorses, under the Super 27 program, that their fuel efficiency increased in the range of almost 11%[25] to 14%[25] while payload capacity (crucial for freighters) went up by almost thrice, from 6,800kg carlier to 18,200kg[25], along with a range increase of 300 NM.[25] The re-engining also led to a much better short-field performance with minimum required runway length for take-off rolls getting reduced by 20% along with an increase in short field range of up to 2,200 km[25] translating into additional fuel or payload capacity of 9,000 kg.

The Super 27 program was originally launched in the late 1980s by Valsan Partners, as the 727RE "Quiet 727" and later in 1996 at the Farnborough Airshow by Rohr (a California based nacelle manufacturer) and subsequently spearheaded by BFGoodrich (following the merger of Rohr with BFGoodrich in December 1997). They were charging a net amount of $8 million[25] for re-engining with a pair of brand new JT8D-217/219s as against the $2.8 million required for installation of hush kits.

The Super 27 program had gotten off to a decent start and picked up really well with almost 200[27] odd 727s (orders & options) roped in and enlisted for re-engining. However, somewhere down the road, the program lost its appeal as well as momentum with only 34[27] 727s ultimately getting re-engined (as the 727-200REs as per ch-aviatin.com) as newer, more fuel efficient jets took centre stage and the older 727s ultimately found their way to the boneyard as the relics of a bygone era...

JT8D-200: The Last Act

In the late 1990s, Pratt & Whitney signed an agreement with Texas based Seven Q Seven, an aircraft modification and development firm, to certify the JT8D-200 engine for service on the Boeing 707. The plan was to open the last potential realm of the re-engining market left, for the JT8D-200, which was the 707-derived military aircraft variants. The plan had merit given that there were around 500 military aircrafts, based on the Boeing 707, which were still in-service, including, the USAF's KC-135s, E-8 JSTARS & E-3 Sentries besides NATOs' AWACS (variant of E-8), which would have benefitted tremendously from a re-engining.

Additionally, noise & emission regulations, especially across Europe, were becoming more and more stringent and were threatening to curtail the life span of in-service commercial 707s operating with older JT8Ds, of which, Omega Air (a stakeholder in seven Q seven) was the biggest operator. As per the agreement, the first flight of a modified 707, powered by the JT8D-200 engines, was slated as early as in late 1998.

The JT8D-219 would have been the logical choice and the most preferred candidate for the re-engining program; despite limited potential gains in fuel efficiencies of around 10+%, instead, of the over 20+% gains possible with the CFM56 engine; owing to its relatively lower price tag. However, both the JT8D-219 and the original TF-33/JT3B engines, which powered the original 707 variants, have the same weight and center of gravity and thus would have required minimal wing modification on the 707 airframe, as compared, to extensive modification which would have been required with the CFM56 engines, making it a huge advantage favoring the JT8D-219. The overall program cost of re-engining with the JT8D-219s, thus, would have turned out to be just half the sum which would have been ultimately required, in case of the CFM56 engines.

In 2001, the first 707-300 aircraft, designated as the B707RE and powered by four JT8D-219 engines, started a formal flight test program, as per a Pratt & Whitney company press release, to demonstrate & validate the capabilities of a re-engined 707-300 airframe powered by the JT8D-219 engines. The press release quotes USAF's lead pilot Jim Lunsford remarking after the flight, "The Pratt powered aircraft is so quiet that you wouldn't even know that the engines are running."[30] Desmond McEvaddy, co-owner of Omega Air, commented, "We had SQS join with Pratt to initiate re-engining our aircraft with a modern commercial engine."[30] He further added, "Now we've had this flawless flight test success, we've proven that the 707 re-engined with the latest JT8D can meet or exceed all noise and emissions restrictions, and we hope that both commercial and military users of 707 aircraft worldwide take notice"[30].

Jason Chamberlain, Director of Airlift, Surveillance and Tanker Engine Programs for Pratt & Whitney said, "The JT8D fits neatly into any space where an old TF33 (JT3D) resides, so there is virtually no aircraft modification required with re-engining,"[30] Chamberlain said. "Additionally, obtaining a commercial certification (an FAA supplemental type certificate) will significantly reduce the development cost for 707 re-engining for military customers."[30]

Pratt & Whitney also affirmed in the press release that the 707s, enabled for military missions and re-engined with the JT8D-219, were expected to have a 10% better fuel efficiency than the older JT8Ds. Northrop Grumman and SQS were pushing for the USAF's proposed efforts for re-engining of its E-8C JSTARS aircrafts while the USAF's E-3 Sentry AEW&C aircrafts, acquired in the late 1970s, were also in consideration as potential re-engining candidates.

Northrop Grumman received a $532 million fixed price contract in 2005 to upgrade, modernize & re-engine the USAF's E-8C JSTARS fleet, comprising 19 aircrafts, aimed at increasing the performance, capabilities, reliability and maintainability of the E-8s. In early 2007, Northrop Grumman officially selected Pratt & Whitney's JT8D-219 engines to power the E-8s with SQS to provide the pods in which the engines were to be housed. In December 2008, the first E-8C, powered by the new JT8D-219 engines, undertook its maiden flight which was followed by the receipt of FAA's supplemental type certificate (STC) post re-engining.

However, the program received a major setback in 2009, while the prime contractor Northrop Grumman was still carrying out engine replacement & other upgrades on the E-8s, as the USAF temporarily halted the funding for the E-8 upgrade & modernization program while exploring other, alternate ways to carry out the missions conducted by the E-8s, with the Northrop Grumman-built RQ-4 Global Hawks, prominently figuring into this developing dynamic.

The DoD, however, started receiving flak from the defense lobbyists for halting & delaying the E-8C upgrades using press & media outlets as their mouthpiece. An article published in July 2009 by the Lexington Institute, a defense industry think-tank funded by top U.S. defense primes, and authored by its COO, Loren P. Thompson, directly took on & slammed the pentagon and the USAF for the delays.

An excerpt from the article mentions, "Now, it can't even find money to replace the plane's failing engines. The latter problem is a remarkable example of bureaucratic foot-dragging, when you consider that defense authorizing and appropriations committees in both chambers of Congress have already approved the money... As a result, about once every ten days the Joint Stars fleet has to abort a mission due to malfunctioning engines, and half the time an in-flight emergency is declared. Needless to say, this tends to reduce the readiness of the plane while greatly increasing maintenance bills."[31] "The Air Force's own estimates show that if it replaced the E-8's decrepit engines with new ones, it could avoid about a million dollars a day in maintenance costs. In fact, the replacement program would pay for itself in eight years, and eventually save $10 billion... without new engines, it will probably become unflyable in the next decade."[31]

Within 2 months of the publishing of the article, the program was back on track with the Pentagon Technology Chief having signed a MOU directing the Air Force to "free up funds for the shipments of engines to begin[31]." The engine shipments began in early 2010 following USAF's award of a $223.6 million contract to Northrop for 4 JT8D-219 engines along with associated wing pylons & cowlings but the fate of the beleaguered program was again in crosshairs, as of fall of the year 2010, with Boeing, too, having jumped into the fray as the company was actively pitching a variant of its P-8A Poseidon maritime surveillance aircraft, based on its 737, as a replacement for the E-8Cs, with additional space and the capability to integrate weapon systems onboard the airframe, as the key pivots of its proposal.

Northrop Grumman completed the first official flight of the JSTARS' T-3 testbed, powered by the JT8D-219 engines, in December 2011. However, by the early 2014, the overall talk in Pentagon & defense establishments had shifted towards outright recapitalization of the E-8C platform with an altogether new procurement program, based on a new age, business-jet class platform, for which an RFP was floated and responded to by industry majors, led by, Northrop, Lockheed and Boeing.

However, that too, did not materialize as the USAF was, in effect, averse to the idea of using a single platform for the crucial mission of supporting and coordinating with ground troops for battlefield management in the 21st century and was rather focusing on a broader, networked capabilities-based solution for relevance & usefulness in an evolved battlefield context and the focus, instead, was on the development of advanced battle management systems. The recapitalization of the E-8C, thus, was 'officially' declared dead by 2018.

The E-8C fleet is still flying, with active aircraft retirements having officially begun, with the first E-8C aircraft just retired from a long & illustrious service of 4+ decades in early February 2022, under the National Defense Authorization Act (NDAA) with the USAF poised to retire all E-8C aircrafts through FY2024.

Among other 707 military variants, the KC-135s are currently being replaced actively, in tranches, with the Boeing's KC-46A Pegasus aerial tanker, based on the 767 aircraft platform, under the USAF's KC-X program which entailed procurement of 179 tankers worth $35 billion. The service is actively looking at inducting a radically different, next generation tanker platform by the mid-to-late 2030s, under its Next Generation Aerial Refueling System (NGAS), also dubbed as the KC-Z, as indicated by its funding of the start-up, JetZero's blended-wing-body tanker concept, offering significant advantages over the traditional tube-and-wing design based concept, especially, given the United States' realigned strategic posture marked by an official pivot to Asia and the realignment of overarching focus on near-peer adversaries.

The E-3 Sentry's recapitalization has already been announced officially by the USAF, with the Boeing's 737-based E-7A Wedgetail, created originally by Boeing for Australia, chosen as the official replacement of the USAF's E-3 Sentries, which however, will continue to fly for another decade and will be retired in phases till the new fleet is fully acquired & integrated.

Interestingly, NATO, through its NATO Support & Procurement Agency (NSPA), recently issued the RFI in December 2022 for replacement of its in-service fleet of 14 E-3 AWACS aircrafts with a modern platform, under its Alliance Future Surveillance and Control (AFSC) program, with top U.S. defense primes, namely, Northrop Grumman, Boeing & L-3 Harris and European defense major Saab having already submitted proposals for the same. NATO is scheduled to pick its final shortlists for the AFSC program during the second half of 2023.

It will be interesting to note that these new aircraft platforms, especially, the KC-46A Pegasus and the E-7A Wedgetail, both feature engines from GE Aviation and CFM International respectively. Further, some variants of the E-3 developed for the European allies, especially for France & the U.K., were powered by the CFM56-2 series engines at the very outset of their induction in the early 1980s, wherein, the engine was designated as the F108. The U.S. Navy's E-6 Mercury airborne command post & communications relay platform, based on the 707-300, too, was powered by the CFM56-2A-2 engines originally when it entered service in the late 1980s. The KC-46A is powered by a pair of GE's legendary CF6 engines while the E-7A sports the iconic CFM56 engines, both of which, are still very much in production and have been picked, primarily, for extreme reliability reasons.

Following its legendary JT8D engine, the Pratt & Whitney era, in military variants & special mission aircrafts segment, too, is finally coming to an end after having dominated the skies for almost over half a century...

Chapter XV

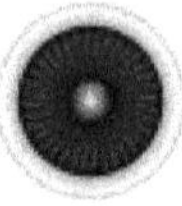

'The Battle of Medium-Thrust Engines'

The global commercial aircraft engines market, in some particular ways, somehow behaves like the geopolitical arena, as witnessed in Europe during the medieval times & even later and that behavior is characterized & captured perfectly by the term 'balance of power', wherein, to check the belligerence and significant rise in political & military power of a particular European state, a number of other European states would come together, combine forces and form a politico-military alliance to collectively balance the power of that state and the overall developing power dynamic as well as equation. It happened with France in the early 19th century during the Napoleonic era and subsequently with Imperial Germany from late 19th century leading up to the onset of World War I.

A similar saga has played out periodically in the global market for commercial aircraft engines, wherein, to balance the strong & dominant position of an engine OEM, in a particular market segment or on a specific aircraft program, other engine OEMs would combine forces, to form either an alliance or a JV, to create a worthy engine competitor in order to take on that 'powerhouse', thereby, trying to create a level playing field for everyone.

The reason behind the success & preference for this particular approach in the commercial engines market is the high cost of development of new engine programs along with high degree of risks associated with the development of new, complex technologies besides the need for a significant maintenance, repair & overhaul (MRO) network with the requisite capacity to service those engines. By forming an alliance, the development costs as well as the associated financial & technological risks and overall investment outlay required, could be shared and reduced considerably.

Creation of International Aero Engines (IAE) to Take-on CFMI

The rise of the CFM56 program, at the onset of the 1980s decade, made other engine makers, especially Pratt & Whitney, who had been the virtually unchallenged market leader in the narrow body aircraft market for almost

2 decades. Further, commercial aviation market had started witnessing rapid growth in passenger traffic following the U.S. market deregulation in 1978.

To challenge the market dominance of CFM56, a consortium of other engine OEMs, led by Pratt & Whitney, formed a JV in the early 1980s, which was named as International Aero Engines (IAE) and originally had 5 engine makers as partners, namely, Pratt & Whitney, Rolls Royce, MTU Aero Engines, Japanese Aero Engines and Fiat-Avio (which later withdrew but stayed with the alliance (Avio) as a supplier). The IAE was registered in Switzerland in 1983 and was headquartered at East Hartford, Connecticut in Pratt & Whitney's backyard. All 4 partners (following Fiat's exit) originally had a 25% ownership share in it.

Prior to the creation of IAE, Rolls Royce and the Japanese Aero Engine Corporation (JAEC) had collaborated briefly in the late 1970s, to co-develop an engine with a thrust output of 20,000 lbf to power the Boeing 737's second generation, the 737-300 Classic series, and McDonnell Douglas' MD-80 programs. The engine was designated as RJ500 and featured a 60 inch, single-stage fan along with an oblate shaped engine nacelle to meet the low ground clearance requirement of the 737. Further, two engine prototypes of the RJ500 were also built and ground tested but the program was ultimately shelved in the early 1980s paving the way for the creation of IAE.

The IAE's raison d'etre was to develop a new, high bypass medium-thrust turbofan engine to power short-to-medium haul narrow body aircrafts with a seating capacity of up to 150 seats, as this was the segment which was projected to register rapid growth over domestic routes, following market deregulation in the U.S. The first engine program from the JV entered market in March 1983, 6 years after the formation of IAE, and was aptly termed as V2500 with the initial Roman numeral 'V' denoting the five original, founding partners of the alliance while 2500 stood for the 25,000 lbf thrust which the original engine version, V2500-A1, was to produce. The bypass ratio of the V2500-A1 was 5.4:1 and it was launched in 1983, which was just in time for the launch of the Airbus' first narrow body aircraft program, the A320, a year later in 1984.

A successful market entry for the V2500 engine program within 6 years of the JV's creation was an achievement in itself as Pratt & Whitney engineer & program manager for the JT8D & JT3D engine programs, Jack Connors, who himself was a part of the leadership team derived from alliance partners, which formed the IAE in London in 1983, has mentioned in his book, "Engines of Pratt & Whitney: A Technical History"[6]. He has mentioned, "This was (referring to V2500 program) a considerable accomplishment as the critics held out no hope that seven companies (considering 3 Japanese companies separately rather than a combined Japanese engine consortium) could get together and produce an engine that the airlines would buy. Well, the critics were wrong. IAE managed to break into the Airbus A320 series aircraft, even though it got there just a little over a year later than the first aircraft powered by the CFM56."[6]

The Airbus' A320 offered an option of two engines for operators to choose from with the first one being the CFM56-5 series and the second one being the IAE's V2500-A1 engine. CFMI initially chose to derive the CFM56-4 series, from its original CFM56-2 engine series, to power the Airbus' A320 aircraft family. The CFM56-4 series was also to compete directly with the RJ500 engine being developed by Rolls Royce-Japanese Aero Engine Corporation (JAEC), prior to IAE.

The CFM56-4 was to produce a thrust output of 25,000 lbf while featuring a larger 68-inch fan, a new low pressure compressor and the new Full Authority Digital Engine Controller (FADEC). The CFM56-4 was unveiled in 1984 for the A320 aircraft family and went up directly against the V2500-A1 which, too, had been launched.

CFM International, however, soon realized that the CFM56-4 was not a match for the V2500-A1 and the company went back to the drawing board to ultimately come up with the new CFM56-5 series, featuring engine variants with thrust output ranging from 22,000 lbf to 34,000 lbf, to power different members of the A320 aircraft family. The CFM56-5A engine variant, with thrust output ranging from 22,000 lbf to 26,500 lbf, powered the Airbus' A320 and A319 aircraft programs while the further improved, CFM56-5B series, with thrust output ranging from 22,000 lbf to 33,000 lbf, was developed to power the larger, A321 variant initially, but went on to power every member of the A320 aircraft family ultimately. The CFM56-5B series featured a further reduction in emissions with the option of a double-annual combustor, usage of a new fan in a longer case and incorporation of a new, low pressure compressor.

The initial engine variants, which powered the A320 program, the CFM56-5-A1 and the V2500-A1, had a thrust output of 25,000 lbf each. Theoretically, the V2500-A1 promised a relatively, slightly better fuel burn rate, measured in Thrust Specific Fuel Consumption (TSFC), than the CFM56-5A1. However, reliability issues experienced by operators with the early stage engines along with limited thrust output of 25,000 lbf, which was incapable of powering the larger A321, forced IAE to develop the V2500-A5, featuring an airflow increase through a slight increase in fan diameter and addition of a booster stage, leading to an increased thrust output of 33,000 lbf.

The V2500-A5 variant, though, was developed primarily for the A321 program, however, its improved reliability & market success, led IAE to start developing & offering de-rated variants of the −A5 for usage on the A320 & A319 programs, translating into benefits for operators emanating from engine hardware commonality across aircraft programs of the A320 family.

The V2500-A5, in fact, proved to be 4% more fuel efficient than its rival CFMI's initial engine variant, the CFM56-5A1, when the two are compared on thrust specific fuel consumption (TSFC) with V2500−A5's TSFC measured at 0.574[32] and CFM56-5A1's pegged at 0.596[32] lb/lbf/h respectively. However, the TSFC of the CFM56-5B4 variant, which powered the A320-214, was even lower at just 0.545 creating an effective overmatch for the CFM56 over V2500.

The availability of the V2500, as a capable & worthy competitor in the early 1980s, effectively led to the onset of the 'battle of medium-thrust engines', between the incumbent CFM56 and the challenger V2500, in the global narrow body aircraft market which were somewhat akin to the 'Great Engine Wars', which were underway in the military aircraft market through the course of the same decade. The CFM56 program, had the 737 Classic series as its impregnable fortress given its presence as the exclusive engine and had a presence on the Airbus' A320 program as well, as an engine option, while the V2500 was being offered as an engine option on the A320.

The overall equation, however, changed radically when McDonnell Douglas decided to further stretch its MD-88 aircraft program to create the MD-90 series, which was the third generation of the DC-9 series launched in the late 1980s, to compete effectively with the Airbus' A320 aircraft family and the Boeing's 737 Classic generation.

The MD-90 featured[34] multiple upgrades, including, a glass cockpit, an advanced flight deck featuring an electronic flight instrument system, an inertial reference system, LED dot-matrix displays for engine & system monitoring and a pair of modern, high bypass V2500-D5 turbofan engines (with the D5 variant retaining the original configuration of the A5) while using different mounting hardware and accessory gearboxes for installation on the MD-90 along with additional thrust for hot-and-high conditions.

The MD-90 series was launched in 1989, with Delta as the usual & truly loyal launch customer, which placed an order for 50 MD-90s along with an option for another 110 aircrafts which ultimately entered service in 1995 on domestic routes across the U.S. market.

McDonnell Douglas, in fact, had also created a further stretch of its MD-80 series in late 1986, in order to compete with the Boeing's 757, and had dubbed it as the MD-90X. This new derivative aircraft, the MD-90X, was capable of seating 180 passengers and offered a choice of engine options to operators, who could choose between the CFM56-5 series and the V2500.

The launch of the MD-90 series, thus, theoretically created a level playing field, both for the CFM56 and the V2500 engine programs, which now had exclusive positions on the 737 and MD-90 series respectively along with a presence on the A320 as an engine option. However, the analogy is relatively limited in scale as well as impact, given that the MD-90 was no 737 and McDonnell Douglas was no Boeing in the commercial aircraft market, especially in the post-Cold

War era, which was just about to dawn upon the world towards the end of the 1980s decade.

The post-Cold War decade of the 1990s weakened McDonnell Douglas Corporation (MDC) significantly with massive defense spending cuts by the United States and the Department of Defense, following the end of Cold War, which triggered a wave of industry consolidation marked by a huge spike in M&As. The MD-90 series, thus, had a very short lifespan, unlike its predecessors, with only 116 aircrafts produced & delivered between the type's entry into service in 1995 and the end of production in 2000 after Boeing's acquisition of McDonnell Douglas in 1997.

Boeing's acquisition of the MDC, which effectively turned the global commercial aircraft market into a duopoly and confined the battle of engines in the commercial aviation market to A320 vs. 737 arch-rivalry, which is very much in place & duly sustained, in an altogether new form, even after 3+ decades of its genesis in the mid-1980s (more on that in the next part of this two-part book series).

V2500's Success – Outcomes & Implications for the IAE Partners

The outright success of the V2500 engine in the narrow body aircraft market had strategic implications for the stakeholders involved in the program as well as rivals. For Pratt & Whitney, the success of the V2500 provided it with a much-needed, continued access to the global narrow body aircraft market, after its legendary JT8D engine had become more or less irrelevant from a competitive perspective, by the end of 1980s. The V2500 formed the second tier of Pratt & Whitney's two-pronged strategy for the narrow body propulsion market, with the first one being the extension of the life span of the JT8D program, through to the turn of the century with the creation of the JT8D-200 series.

For Rolls Royce, the creation of the IAE and the V2500 engine program provided it with the highly desired access to the commercial aircraft market which had been thwarted effectively by Pratt & Whitney twice earlier. As discussed earlier, the first effort was made by Rolls Royce in the late 1950s with its Conway, which was blocked by Pratt & Whitney (which had just launched its JT3D program). The second attempt was made in the early 1960s, when Rolls Royce's Spey engine had been finalized by Boeing for its 727 program but Pratt & Whitney staged a coup, which led to the creation of the JT8D and kept Rolls Royce out of the narrow body market.

For CFM International, the IAE was a potent rival & the V2500 a worthy competitor, which kept the company on its toes throughout, in terms, of tactical responsiveness by driving its relative evolution & progression of its products & technologies and ensuring market responsiveness through enhanced capability, accessibility as well as capacity of its MRO network.

Another important question to be asked in this context is 'what makes for a successful JV?' especially in a highly technology intensive and complex industry, such as aviation gas turbine engines. An investigation into the key success factors behind the sustained success of CFM International JV by two INSEAD researchers in their research paper titled, "When Uncommon Alliances Provide a Fast Response to Disruption"[35], just published in June 2023, reveals the answer, "When considering and researching successful long-lasting alliances such as CFM or the collaboration between ST Microelectronics and Hewlett Packard on printers' cartridges, and many others in which we observe a common pattern. They rely on converging strategic intents, complementarity and co-specialization between partners' resources, dedicated teams, strong leadership, authenticity, fairness, an intelligent design for sharing costs, risks, and benefits, a focus on on-boarding all layers in the partners' organizations and showing sensitivity to different cultures"[35].

The authors unravel the essence and drive home the message effectively with their concluding remarks, "But also, and most critically, they take time to take off and bring benefits. To be able to evolve and adapt to unforeseen developments, good or bad, they then require a high level of trust between the partners, and the confidence they will act in their mutual interests rather than attempt to seek one-sided advantage from the collaboration. In alliances, trust results from reliability in delivering against commitments from mutual forbearance in interactions once something has been put at risk. Thus, it slowly emerges from interaction and collaboration experiences with growing mutual dependence being accepted over time."[35]

Hope CFMI rivals are tuned in and listening intently...

Chapter XVI

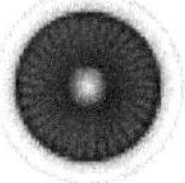

The 'Phantom Plane' with 'Alien Tech'

Boeing had been studying the prospects of launching a new, clean sheet aircraft program extensively in the mid-1980s, designated initially as 7-7 and later 7J7, targeted at the short & medium haul aircraft segment, with a 150-seat capacity, and aimed directly at Airbus which had just launched its A320 program. Additionally, Boeing's 757 had just entered service in 1983 and had received a weak market reception from the airlines, which had, instead, been leaning towards smaller aircrafts in a deregulated U.S. market environment of the 1980s which had given a huge boost to demand for small narrow body aircrafts, including the 737, MD-80 and the A320.

Termed 7J7, the program had been elaborately conceived for domestic operations and was to be powered by an exotic propulsion technology, known as propfan, which promised delivering an almost 40% improvement in fuel consumption, as compared to conventional turbofan engines of the generation, with similar specifications. However, pitching fuel efficiency as a key proposition was quite incongruous in a low crude oil price environment of the 1980s, in which, oil prices had virtually plummeted after skyrocketing during the oil crisis of the 1970s.

Boeing's 7J7 in the 1980s Market Landscape

The 1980s had, in fact, been a chaotic decade for the industry with oil prices abruptly changing polarity and plummeting, led by an OPEC supply glut, which in turn, improved airlines profitability. Further, the deregulation of the airlines industry in the U.S. market in 1978 opened the market floodgates and brought in a number of new players, including, start-ups which led to massive changes in market landscape, including, a significant increase in competitive intensity.

To capitalize on the same, Airbus had launched its A320 narrow body in the mid-1980s incorporating a range of next generation technologies. The centre of gravity of Boeing's product strategy focus & game plan, back in the early 1980s, had been the middle of the market with its latest-pair of clean sheet aircraft twins, the 757 & 767, having just entered service in the early 1980s to take on the Airbus A300 & A310 respectively.

The 7J7 (the 7-7 originally) program had been conceived by Boeing in 1983, aimed originally as a replacement for the ageing 727 trijet, which was almost on the verge of being retired. It would have created a gap in Boeing's product portfolio between the single-aisle 737, which was the entry level jet, and the 757, positioned right in the middle of the market. The point was relevant given that the 737-100, the smallest aircraft of the 737 Original series, had a seating capacity of 118 passengers while the larger 757-200 had really long legs & could easily carry over 200 passengers across the Atlantic from the U.S.' East Coast.

Further, in a deregulated market environment of the 1980s in the U.S., smaller aircrafts were thriving and gaining ground over larger ones with the economics favoring them. It resulted in the weak market debut of the 757 which had just entered service in early 1983. The 757 was followed by the first member of the 737 Classic series, the 737-300's EIS, in late 1984.

The 150 seat 7J7, thus, hypothetically would have filled the emerging void in the portfolio perfectly. Additionally, Scandinavian Airlines (SAS) was looking to replace its fleet of DC-9s at the time and knocked at Boeing's door for a potential aircraft concept for a replacement and conveyed its eagerness to be the launch customer, which made Boeing even more inclined to pursue of the 7J7 program.

Theoretically, at the outset, Boeing was looking at 7J7, simply as a 727 replacement, in its aircraft line-up with plans for a similar seating capacity of around 150, a similar operating range of around 2250+ NM (with the 7J7 base variant), a similar MTOW of around 160,000 lb -170,000 lb but with a different six or seven-abreast seating layout in a twin aisle configuration.

However, with the higher gross weight variant, Boeing was almost heading towards the middle of the market, targeting the operating range of the 757 at almost 4000+ NM with a six-abreast seating configuration. The fuselage width on the 7J7 was also being planned to be almost 15% to 30% more than the 727.

The 7J7 concept, in terms of specifications which were unveiled in August 1987, closely matched the A320, which had been launched just a couple of years back in 1984 with a similar MTOW of 172,000 lb, a typical 2-class seating of 150 passengers but with a longer operating range of 3,300 nmi.

However, dimensionally, the 7J7 concept was positioned somewhere beyond the A320 & closer to its larger sibling, the A321, which was non-existent at the time and was yet to be launched by Airbus. However, the 7J7's wing span & wing area were dimensionally even larger than the A321, based on the initial specifications released in August 1987.

Propfan Engines and the 7J7

Boeing, evidently, was looking for an overmatch over the A320, in terms of technological superiority by incorporating, newer engines known as propfans, which were way more fuel efficient than conventional turbofans. Robert R. Waggener, Boeing's customer manager at the time, mentioned in an interview (given in 1986) about propfan technology, "The technology that will be ready by 1989 (referring to the A320) will make an aircraft 9% cheaper (with latest conventional turbofans) to run than today's airliners. By 1992, the improvement could be up to 60% (referring to propfans powered 7J7)."[41]

A propfan powered 7J7, incorporating cutting edge technologies, thus, theoretically could have ruined the business case for the A320; had the propfan technology been commercialized in time & delivered on the projected fuel efficiency gains, noise levels & overall reliability; and it could, in turn, have been Boeing's befitting reply to the A320, especially the A321, which was yet to be launched.

However, the decision was subject to the consent of the market forces, which didn't seem too interested at the moment, as oil prices were at rock bottom, noise problems with the propfans had yet to be resolved and their reliability, too, was yet to be demonstrated & proven. Propfans, thus, had a long road ahead of them and were long way away from commercialization.

Boeing's value proposition, with the 7J7, thus, had elicited keen interest in the 7J7 from across the Atlantic in Europe to markets as far as Japan. The Japanese industry, in fact, proposed to even be a strategic investor in the program by signing a letter of understanding to own a 25% stake in the program in 1984, which would have been worth $2 billion at the time and offered to even fund the development as well, if Boeing agreed to power the 7J7 with the IAE's V2500 engine program, which had just been launched and had a major involvement of the Japanese Aero Engine Corporation, as a key program partner.

The Japanese, however, were looking at 1988 as the entry into service timeline for the "YXX" program, as they had termed it. Boeing, however, had other plans in the offing as the company was looking for a technological leap generationally and had almost been smitten by the propfan technology with its enormous potential of double digit fuel savings while looking away from the technological risks & challenges it entailed.

Boeing, ultimately, ruled in favor of propfans over conventional turbofans (rather than offering both as engine options to operators) by choosing the GE's unproven, gearless Unducted Fan (UDF) propulsion system, GE36, for the 7J7, much to Japan's chagrin. The move; which further delayed the proposed entry into service of the 7J7 to 1992; simultaneously also infused significant, unnecessary technology risks into the program as well, given the additional time horizon required for propfan technology's maturation & certification.

Propfan Technology – Magic Wand or the Pandora's Box

Propfans or Open rotor technology; was being touted as the next big thing in aviation in the 1980s and being considered as the radical, generational leap, technologically, in the commercial aviation's eternal quest for evolution. The program had its genesis in 1975, right in the middle of the 1970s oil crisis, under a NASA Aircraft Energy Efficiency aeronautical research program which aimed at potentially developing highly fuel-efficient engine technology for aviation applications, by blending the speed & performance of traditional turbofan engines and the fuel efficiency of turboprops, in order, to address & tackle ongoing volatility in the global crude oil prices.

The oil prices in 1986, following the skyrocketing levels of the 1970s, were at the rock bottom levels of 50-60 cents, which still was almost five-times the level at which they had been prior to the 1973's crisis. However, given their unpredictable trajectory, the aviation industry was avidly looking forward to the almost 30% improvements in fuel efficiency, being promised by the propfan technology, over conventional turbofans.

Propfan technology, essentially entailed a large propeller fan, rotating without being encased by the large, heavy duct with its blades rotating almost virtually at supersonic tip-speed to generate very high-bypass ratios of almost 60:1 which were at the core of the huge fuel efficiency gains being promised by it.

The leading aircraft engine manufacturers in the U.S. had already been pursuing their own R&D programs on propfans, at the onset of the 1980s decade, led by GE's Unducted Fan (UDF) as the GE-36 & the Allison-Pratt & Whitney JV, with its 578-DX engine, with NASA supporting them by sharing the outcomes of its own preliminary research efforts on the technology.

However, managing in-cabin noise was going to be the biggest hurdle, which had to be overcome, before the propfans could make it further to the commercialization stage, which was being expected to be achieved by the industry by 1992. Boeing had gone a step even further and was targeting ambitious fuel efficiency gains of around 60%, on the propfans powered 7J7, with additional fuel efficiency gains expected to be realized from the use of lightweight materials in the airframe, design & development of high lift/low drag wing and incorporation of an advanced flight control system (FCS).

Further, a 1987 NASA document prophetically concluded, "barring other, unforeseen problems, the prop fan airliner could be carrying passengers within five years[42]". However, the heralding of prop fans as the next savior of commercial aviation, in the post-oil crisis world in the 1980s, was not just a regional phenomenon. In fact, a large number of aviation players across continents; including, European players like Fokker, ATR, Aerospatiale & Messerschmitt to the Soviets, led by Tupolev and Ilyushin; were either studying or had already proposed propfans-based commercial aircrafts through the 1980s decade.

The Airbus' take on Prop fans, however, contrasted completely from its North American counterparts, despite the fact that SNECMA, the French engine manufacturer, had already been invested in the development of the UDF technology at the time. It was via CFM International, which had already made a 35% investment in GE's UDF propfan engine program, which was later designated as the GE36.

In fact, SNECMA's reigning chairman in the late 1986, had commented, "The in-development CFM56-5S2 would be the last turbofan created for the CFM56 family, and that there is no point in spending more money on turbofans. UDF is the future[2]". Rolls Royce, the leading British engine manufacturer, too, was very much in the race and had placed its own bet on a wing-mounted propfan concept, designated it as the 'Contrafan'.

There were, however, a lot of technical issues pertaining to the propfan technology, which were yet to be addressed & sorted out before the technology could be deemed as mature and ready for commercialization. The most perturbing & challenging issue with the technology, pertained to managing in-cabin noise levels, as the ductless fan with its carbon fiber blades rotating at supersonic tip speeds, would have created huge noise problems. Besides, there were unexplored issues of structural fatigue caused to the airframe, due to vibration. The prop-fan technology, thus, in order to be successful, had to effectively bring down the noise levels to, at least at par with conventional turbofans, or to the humanly acceptable levels.

Further, the actual mounting position of the propfans was another aspect still left to be pondered upon, as mounting them under the wings would have led to in-cabin noise & structural fatigue problems while mounting them on the rear fuselage would have created interference problems with the wing's air flow.

PropFans and Engine OEMs

Propfan development efforts; being spearheaded at the time by the GE's gearless UDF technology (which created the GE36 prop-fan engine) and the Allison's geared 578-DX engine; continued & ultimately reached the test flights stage. The Allison's propfan concept was mounted on a modified

Gulfstream II aircraft & was tested over 1987-1988. The GE36, developed with 35% participation from SNECMA (now Safran) as an industrial partner, was first flight-tested on a 727-100 test bed in 1986. McDonnell Douglas, which had become a key patron of the propfan technology development effort, mounted the GE36 engine on a modified MD-80 demonstrator aircraft, which was also showcased at the 1988's Farnborough Airshow.

GE claimed that its UDF technology could cover a broad range of power output requirements and was even capable of meeting or surpassing the power output of its CF6 turbofans. The GE36 was planned to be developed in four variants with thrust output ranging from 14,000 lbf (for the MD-91X) to 25,000 lbf (for the MD-92 & 7J7 programs) while a 22,000 lbf variant was to power the MD-91. McDonnell Douglas also tested the Allison's 501-M78 engine on its MD-80 test bed in 1989.

PropFans: An Aerial Chimera

The propfan technology, however, ultimately, never saw the light of commercial service with the judgment passed by the indifferent & impersonal market forces, driven solely by the underlying economics, and their verdict at the time was against it. The cabin noise problem & prevailing low oil price environment questioned the very viability of the idea. Further, all market players involved in the development efforts faced different set of issues which also impeded any further progress on the commercialization of propfans. The Prop fanhype, thus, somehow, was completely in line with the Gartner's Hype Cycle with the 'Peak of Inflated Expectations' followed by the 'Trough of Disillusionment' perfectly!

Boeing, thus, wound up the 7J7 program forever. McDonnell Douglas Corporation (MDC); having launched the MD-90(derived from MD-80) narrow body airliner, powered by the V2500 turbofan in 1989, to take on the A320; too, abandoned its MD-91X, MD-92X & MD-94X variants altogether amid shifting priorities. Al Novick, who was part of the Allison-P&W team which had developed the 501-M78 engine, read out the program's cryptic obituary: "The operation was successful, but the patient died"[43] referring to MDC's abandoning of the development of propfan- powered aircraft programs, post the successful flight of the MD-80 test bed in 1989, powered by the 501-M78 engine.

GE, which had developed the GE36, was initially touting the GE36, as a replacement for the now legendary, CFM56 turbofan engine, which had back then been faring poorly, in terms of sales uptake, during its initial half-a-decade of market introduction in the mid-1970s. However, by the middle-to-late 1980s, the CFM56 program had gained huge sales traction and GE, thus, did not want the program to be cannibalized by the GE36. GE, much akin to Boeing, leveraged the UDF development effort & ultimately injected the UDF's fan blade technology into the GE90 engine program, which eventually found its way into powering the Boeing's 777.

Alan Mulally, Boeing's Director of Engineering for the 7J7 program summarized the UDF story in a nutshell in an interview much later as: "The biggest issue with the UDF was to make it a simple engine and get the reliability up and the maintenance down[43]".

The Propfan saga was more or less over, despite the love of techies for it or CFM International claiming the Open Rotor technology as the future of engines once again during the 2000s decade, given the much stricter noise regulations in place now and the onset of the industry's shift towards sustainability.

It was a crucial lesson, learnt the hard way by Boeing, following the eventual scuttling of the 7J7. Ultimately, the 7J7 program, in which Boeing had invested significant resources towards development, apparently turned out to be more or less an internal developmental exercise with the company eventually setting it advertently on a slow death course with gradual reduction in funding & resource allocation. Following this, Boeing recalibrated its strategy focus & zeroed-down on to the 777 program in 1989, as part of a major & sweeping product strategy shift.

Will the Future once again be PropFans?

Ironically, the propfan/Unducted fan (UDF) technology is all set for resurgence in a modern, futuristic avatar, in order, to tackle the significant problem of climate change. CFM International partners, GE Aviation &

Safran, have once again been re-working on this radical technology and have termed their next propulsion technology development effort as, RISE, which is an acronym for Revolutionary Innovation for Sustainable Engines (RISE).

CFM International mentions that its next generation engine, likely to be available in 2035, would be based on technology matured through the RISE program featuring an open fan based architecture and it will be capable of reducing fuel consumption as well as CO_2 emissions by almost 20% as compared to today's best engines...

Stay tuned for more on that in Part 2 of this aerial expedition...

Bibliography

1. "Soviets Shoot Down Jet in 1960 U-2 Incident", LA Times Archive, April 30, 1990 From Associated Press

https://www.latimes.com/archives/la-xpm-1990-04-30-mn-120-story.html

2. "Powers Down: The 60th Anniversary Of The U-2 Spy Plane Incident", Radio Free Europe, Radio Liberty, May 01, 2020, By Kateryna Oliynvk & Stuart Greer [1]

https://www.rferl.org/a/sixty-years-ago-the-soviet-union-shot-down-u-s-spy-plane/30585501.html

3. Pratt & Whitney's TF33 Engine https://prattwhitney.com/products-and-services/products/military-engines/tf33

4. National Air & Space Museum https://airandspace.si.edu/collection-objects/pratt-whitney-jt3d-1-production-prototype-turbofan-engine/nasm_A19721331000

5. Rolls Royce Spey https://www.rolls-royce.com/products-and-services/defence/aerospace/combat-jets/spey.aspx

6. The Engines of Pratt & Whitney: A Technical History, Jack Connors, ISBN[2] 978 1 60086[3]

7. "Giant Jets Pose Giant Problems" By Marylin Bender, April 09, 1972 New York Times https://www.nytimes.com/1972/04/09/archives/giant-jets-pose-giant-problems-too-many-passengers-or-too-few-can.html

---

1. https://www.rferl.org/a/sixty-years-ago-the-soviet-union-shot-down-u-s-spy-plane/30585501.html

2. https://en.wikipedia.org/wiki/ISBN_(identifier)

3. https://en.wikipedia.org/wiki/Special:BookSources/978%2B1%2B60086%2B711%2B8

8. "Mounting Troubles", By Lee S. Langston, The American Society of Mechanical Engineers, March 2011, 133(03): 46-49 (4 pages) https://asmedigitalcollection.asme.org/memagazineselect/article/133/03/46/380174/Mounting-TroublesThe-First-Jumbo-Jet-was-an

9. 1972 Social Security Amendments, By Robert M. Ball, https://www.ssa.gov/history/1972amend.html

10. William Greider. "Secrets of the Temple: How the Federal Reserve Runs the Country." Simon and Schuster, 1989.

11. The Standard Reference of U.S. Scheduled Air Transportation Official Publication of the Air Transport Association of America https://airlines.org/wp-content/uploads/2014/08/1970.pdf

12. Oil Price History – Highs & Lows Since 1970 https://www.thebalancemoney.com/oil-price-history-3306200

13. Power to Fly: An Engineer's Life, Brian H. Rowe, Martin Ducheny, November 2004

14. The Noisy Dawn of the Jet Age, Sound & Vibration Magazine, January 2007 Issue, Page 94 http://www.sandv.com/downloads/0701bera2.pdf

15. International Civil Aviation Organization (ICAO) https://www.icao.int/publications/pages/doc7300.aspx

16. S.3279 - Aircraft and Airport Noise Reduction Act 95th Congress (1977-1978), Congress.gov https://www.congress.gov/bill/95th-congress/senate-bill/3279

17. Pratt & Whitney J57 Engine, Aviation History http://www.aviation-history.com/engines/j57.htm

18. Aircraft Noise Levels for U.S. Certified & Foreign Aircrafts, Federal Aviation Administration (FAA) https://www.faa.gov/about/office_org/headquarters_offices/apl/noise_emissions/aircraft_noise_levels/

19. https://web.archive.org/web/20110629014517/http://www.boeing.com/defense-space/military/kc135-strat/index.html

20. CFM56-7B Offers Reliability, Life Extension for Boeing 707 Platforms https://www.cfmaeroengines.com/press-articles/cfm56-7b-offers-reliability-life-extension-for-boeing-707-platforms/

21. "Delta's Long-Lasting DC-8s", KEY.AERO, February 09, 2021 by Barry Lloyd https://www.key.aero/article/deltas-long-lasting-dc-8s

22. Airline Deregulation by Alfrad E. Kahn, The Concise Encyclopedia of Economics (CEE), Library of Economics & Liberty https://www.econlib.org/library/Enc1/AirlineDeregulation.html

23. Getting to Grips with ETOPS, EADS N.V., Issue V – October 1998 http://www.737ng.co.uk/AIRBUS%20ETOPS%20Guide.pdf

24. "Pratt & Whitney's Workhorse", The New York Times, September 20, 1985, By Agis Salpukas https://www.nytimes.com/1985/09/20/business/pratt-whitney-s-workhorse.html

25. "Sound Solutions", By Guy Norris, Flight Global, July 14, 1999 https://www.flightglobal.com/sound-solutions/27606.article

26. "AZAL CFM56-5B Order Valued at $45 Million", CFM Aero Engines, September 1, 2004

https://www.cfmaeroengines.com/press-articles/azal-cfm56-5b-order-valued-at-45-million/

27. "Did you know about the Boeing 727's Re-Engining Program?" By Chris Loh, Simple Flying, Published February 07, 2022

https://simpleflying.com/boeing-727-re-engining-program/

28. "JT9D-200 by MTU Aero Engines", https://www.mtu.de/engines/commercial-aircraft-engines/narrowbody-and-regional-jets/jt8d-200/

29. The JT8D Engine by Pratt & Whitney https://www.prattwhitney.com/en/products/commercial-engines/jt8d

30. "What happened to 707RE with JT8D-219?", Key Aero, February 18, 2007 by Multirole re-posting the Pratt & Whitney's original company press release dated August 21, 2001. https://www.key.aero/forum/modern-military-aviation/69499-what-happened-to-707re-with-jt8d-219

31. "Air Force Delay on Radar Plane Fix Hurts Soldiers", The Lexington Institute, July 29, 2009 http://www.lexingtoninstitute.org/air-force-delay-on-radar-plane-fix-hurts-soldiers?a=1&c=1129

https://www.defenseindustrydaily.com/Re-engining-the-E-8-JSTARS-04891/

32. Civil Jet Aircraft Design By L. Jenkinson, P. Simpkin and D. Rhodes, https://booksite.elsevier.com/9780340741528/appendices/data-b/table-1/default.htm

33. "CFM56 Engines: The Standard to which others are judged", CFM International Press Release, September 02, 1996

https://www.cfmaeroengines.com/press-articles/cfm56-engines-the-standard-to-which-others-are-judged/

34. Boeing: Historical Snapshot – MD-80/MD-90 Commercial Transports   https://www.boeing.com/history/products/md-80-and-md-90-commercial-transport.page

35. "When Uncommon Alliances Provide a Fast Response to Disruption", INSEAD Working Paper No. 2023/26/STR by Yves L. Doz and Bart De Roover published by SSRN June 13, 2023

https://papers.ssrn.com/sol3/papers.cfm?abstract_id=4477122

36. Recession of 1981-82, July 1981-November 1982, Federal Reserve History, By Tim Sablik, Federal Reserve Bank of Richmond https://www.federalreservehistory.org/essays/recession-of-1981-82

37. "New Jumbo Jet Engines are planned by Pratt", By Richard Witkin, December 09, 1982, The New York Times https://www.nytimes.com/1982/12/09/business/new-jumbo-jet-engines-are-planned-by-pratt.html

38. RAF celebrates 10 years of service with CFM56-2 –powered E-3D AWACS Fleet https://www.cfmaeroengines.com/press-articles/raf-celebrates-10-years-of-service-with-cfm56-2-powered-e-3d-awacs-fleet/

39. Taking Off: What the Anniversary of the America's First Jet Engine Means for the Future of Flight https://blog.geaerospace.com/technology/taking-off-what-the-anniversary-of-americas-first-jet-engine-means-for-the-future-of-flight/

40. A Strategist with Insight: Remembering Jim Krebs, Aerospace Visionary who helped Launch GE into the Jet Age

https://www.ge.com/news/reports/a-strategist-with-insight-remembering-jim-krebs-aerospace-visionary-who-helped-launch-ge

41. "Joint venture brings back propellers", New Scientist, March 13, 1986, By Helen Gavaghan, Accessed via Google Books https://books.google.co.in/ books?id=mYVNkaEJpz4C&pg=PA27&redir_esc=y#v=onepage&q&f=fa [4]

42. Spinoff, National Aeronautics and Space Administration (NASA), Office of Commercial Programs Technology Utilization Division, James Haggerty, August 1987, NTRS https://ia801204.us.archive.org/5/items/ NASA_NTRS_Archive_19880002195/ NASA_NTRS_Archive_19880002195.pdf

43. "The short, happy life of the prop-fan", Air & Space Magazine, Bill Sweetman, Published September 2005 https://www.airspacemag.com/history-of-flight/the-short-happy-life-of-the-prop-fan-7856180/?all

44. "GE1 'Building Block' Engine: Greatest GE Engine Ever?", https://blog.geaerospace.com/100-year-anniversary/ge1-building-block-engine-greatest-ge-jet-engine-ever/

---

4. https://books.google.co.in/ books?id=mYVNkaEJpz4C&pg=PA27&redir_esc=y#v_43ec3e5dee6e706af7766fffea512721_onepage_6 cff047854f19ac2aa52aac51bf3af4a_q_6cff047854f19ac2aa52aac51bf3af4a_f_43ec3e5dee6e706af7766fffe a512721_false

About the Author

Rajat Narang is the Co-Founder & Partner of Noealt Corporate Services, a niche Research Firm pivoted on the Global Aerospace & Defense Industry since 2009, apart from being an Aerospace & Defense (A&D) Industry Researcher & Specialist, Serial Author and Nuclear, Aviation & Cold-War Historian.

He is a member of the 'World Institute for Nuclear Security' (WINS), a leading non-governmental organisation headquartered in Vienna, Austria which works closely with the International Atomic Energy Agency (IAEA) towards nuclear security. He is also associated with the 'International Campaign for Abolishment of Nuclear Weapons (ICAN)', based in Geneva, which won the Nobel Peace Prize in 2017 for its efforts besides being associated with the U.S.-based 'Beyond Nuclear' and 'Nuclear Threat Initiative' which have been spearheading anti-nuclear activism for decades.

He has authored over 2000+ syndicated research reports since 2009 and has authored almost 20 non-fiction books on Commercial & Military Aviation, Nuclear & Cold War History and Leadership. The end users of his reports have been senior executives of leading A&D Industry OEMs, led by Airbus, Boeing, Bombardier, Embraer, Gulfstream, Dassault, Textron Aviation and their supplier base, including, engine OEMs and T-1 suppliers, such as, GE Aviation, Rolls Royce, Pratt & Whitney, Safran & Spirit Aerosystems. His reports have also been leveraged by the U.S. Air Force, U S Navy & top global defense primes, including, Lockheed Martin Corporation, BAE Systems, General Dynamics Land Systems, RTX and Korean Aerospace Industries (KAI).

His educational background includes a Masters in Business Administration (MBA) in International Business with Business Strategy as the core pivot followed by a Masters in Political Science with specialization in International Relations. He has further pursued advanced, short learning programs from leading Global Universities & Institutions, including, IAEA's Nuclear Safety Overview, Nuclear Arms Control, Politics & Economics of International Energy from Sciences Po and Changing Global Order, Terrorism &

Counter-Terrorism & the International Law in Action Series from the Leiden University.

Currently, he is pursuing the Stanford University's flagship program, "Living at the Nuclear Brink: Yesterday & Today", conducted jointly by eminent scientists from the Los Alamos National Laboratory, which produced the world's first Nuclear weapons, and Dr. William J. Perry, who served as the 19th U.S. Secretary of Defense under President Bill Clinton from 1994 to 1997, wherein, he was the chief architect of post-Cold War U.S. Nuclear Doctrine, Posture & Policies and worked actively towards arms & force reduction efforts across both sides in the post Cold War-era.

Being truly passionate about Naval Aviation & the A&D Industry and having almost made the cut to be a Naval Aviator; following a selection by the Naval Academy in the late 1990s, A&D continues to be the core pivot of his professional pursuits even to this day.

Bitten early by the A&D, Strategy & Nuclear bugs; he has been avidly & actively tracking, following and pursuing them for over 2+ decades.

His blog, 'The Radioactive Warzone', focused on the A&D Industry and all things Nuclear, is accessible at https://www.noealtcorporateservices.com/blog-list